Social Cohesion Contested

OFF THE FENCE: MORALITY, POLITICS, AND SOCIETY

The series is published in partnership with the
Centre for Applied Philosophy,
Politics & Ethics (CAPPE), University of Brighton.

Series Editors:
Bob Brecher, Professor of Moral Philosophy, University of Brighton
Robin Dunford, Senior Lecturer in Globalisation
and War, University of Brighton
Michael Neu, Senior Lecturer in Philosophy,
Politics and Ethics, University of Brighton

Off the Fence presents short, sharply argued texts in applied moral and political philosophy, with an interdisciplinary focus. The series constitutes a source of arguments on the substantive problems that applied philosophers are concerned with: contemporary real-world issues relating to violence, human nature, justice, equality and democracy, self and society. The series demonstrates applied philosophy to be at once rigorous, relevant, and accessible—philosophy-in-use.

The Right of Necessity: Moral Cosmopolitanism and Global Poverty, by Alejandra Mancilla

Complicity: Criticism between Collaboration and Commitment, by Thomas Docherty

The State and the Self: Identity and Identities, by Maren Behrensen

Just Liberal Violence: Sweatshops, Torture, War, by Michael Neu

The Troubles with Democracy, by Jeff Noonan

Against Borders: Why the World Needs Free Movement of People, by Alex Sager

Digital Working Lives: Worker Autonomy and the Gig Economy, by Time Christiaens

The Other Enlightenment: Race, Sexualist and Self-Estrangement, by Matthew Sharpe

University in Crisis: From the Middle Ages to the University of Excellence, by Michael Schapira

Social Cohesion Contested, by Dan Swain and Petr Urban

Social Cohesion Contested

Dan Swain and Petr Urban

ROWMAN & LITTLEFIELD
Lanham • Boulder • New York • London

Published by Rowman & Littlefield
An imprint of The Rowman & Littlefield Publishing Group, Inc.
4501 Forbes Boulevard, Suite 200, Lanham, Maryland 20706
www.rowman.com
86-90 Paul Street, London EC2A 4NE

Copyright © 2024 by The Rowman & Littlefield Publishing Group, Inc.

All rights reserved. No part of this book may be reproduced in any form or by any electronic or mechanical means, including information storage and retrieval systems, without written permission from the publisher, except by a reviewer who may quote passages in a review.

British Library Cataloguing in Publication Information Available

Library of Congress Cataloging-in-Publication Data

Names: Swain, Dan, author. | Urban, Petr, 1977– author.
 Title: Social cohesion contested / Dan Swain and Petr Urban.
 Description: Lanham : Rowman & Littlefield Publishers, [2024] | Series: Off the fence: Morality, politics and society | Includes bibliographical references and index. | Summary: "Oversimplification of the concept of social cohesion as a singularly identifiable marker of social growth has lead to obscured understanding of the nuances necessary for achievement of the term's true potential. This book thus provides a critique of a popular concept and an example of engaged philosophical criticism of social research and policy"— Provided by publisher.
 Identifiers: LCCN 2023041170 (print) | LCCN 2023041171 (ebook) | ISBN 9781538176627 (cloth) | ISBN 9781538176641 (ebook)
 Subjects: LCSH: Social participation. | Social integration. | Social sciences—Research.
 Classification: LCC HM711 .S93 2024 (print) | LCC HM711 (ebook) | DDC 302/.14—dc23/eng/20231019
 LC record available at https://lccn.loc.gov/2023041170
 LC ebook record available at https://lccn.loc.gov/2023041171

For Julita and Hana

Contents

Acknowledgments	ix
Introduction	xi
Chapter 1: Staking Out the Terrain: Key Trends and Distinctions in Social Cohesion	1
Chapter 2: From Radars to Regimes: Concepts of Social Cohesion in Focus	19
Chapter 3: Between Economic Growth and Social Rights: European Policy Discourse	39
Chapter 4: Exporting Cohesive Societies: Social Cohesion and International Development	57
Chapter 5: Contesting Social Cohesion	75
Notes	93
Bibliography Part A: Policy Literature	119
Bibliography Part B: Research Literature	123
Index	131
About the Authors	137

Acknowledgments

This book would not have been possible without the encouragement and support of the *Off the Fence* series editors Bob Brecher and Robin Dunford. We benefited from their thoughtful comments and suggestions throughout the entire process of writing this book. We are also grateful for valuable feedback, at various stages of the project, from our colleagues Alexander Bryan, Emanuela Ceva, Geoffrey Dierckxsens, Joe Grim Feinberg, Matteo Gianni, Andrej Grubačic, Tomáš Hříbek, Juraj Hvorecký, Adriana Jesenková, Alice Sjöström Koubová, Jan Maršálek, Jiří Šafr, Areti Theofilopoulu, Joan Tronto, and Pavel Urban, as well as participants of the GECOPOL seminar at University of Geneva on 16 May 2023, and audiences at the Department of Philosophy at Pavol Jozef Šafárik University in Košice and the Department of Philosophy at Matej Bel University in Banská Bystrica on 13–14 June 2023. Last but not least, we want to thank Natalie Mandziuk at Rowman and Littlefield for her support and hard work on this project.

This book is an outcome of the project "Towards a New Ontology of Social Cohesion" (Czech Science Foundation grant nr. GA19–20031S) realized at the Institute of Philosophy of the Czech Academy of Sciences.

Introduction

A popular narrative about the COVID-19 pandemic goes as follows. In the early days of the outbreak, previously divided societies united in the face of a common challenge. In Britain, people voluntarily stayed home and clapped for the NHS. In the Czech Republic, where the present authors are based, a small cottage industry developed making and distributing homemade masks. Mutual aid groups arose to support those in need, and disparate social groups united against a common enemy. This, however, did not last long. As the reality of a second wave hit home, and politicians began to make decisions ranging from the unpopular to the incompetent, tensions returned, sharper than ever before. Vaccine hesitancy and conspiracy theories revealed a deep mistrust of institutions, and unity gave way to conflict, suspicion, and mutual recrimination. Whatever divisions had briefly been healed were reopened. A report from IPSOS thus insists, "There is no question that the pandemic created a more 'cohesive' society in many countries in its early days. People will always pull together when there is a common enemy. . . . But our COVID-19 tracking surveys have suggested that social cohesion has started to fray as the pandemic has evolved."[1] A similar report from the British Academy echoes this, suggesting that "there is clear empirical evidence that social cohesion and community solidarity grew across the UK at the start of the COVID-19 pandemic" but "measures of people's sense of division and unity across the UK indicate that feelings of unity subsided from May onward and by September [2020] had returned to slightly above pre-pandemic levels, with only 15% saying that the UK was becoming more united."[2] Such reports give a name to whatever it was that rose and then fell: *social cohesion*.

Following the pandemic, social cohesion is firmly back on the agenda. The World Economic Forum's 2022 *Global Risks Report* identified "social cohesion erosion" as a major perceived threat, with its Global Risks Survey ranking it the fourth highest concern (the highest not directly related to climate change and environmental crisis) and the one that has grown the most since the pandemic.[3] This reflects real and growing concerns about the stability and sustainability of contemporary forms of life, but also groups these concerns together and articulates them as a single threat, represented as the erosion or depletion of a particular resource or substance.[4]

It is this way of talking about social cohesion that we want to challenge in this book. This is not because we don't care about whether societies are holding together or not, nor because we do not think there are major crises that put into question the sustainability of our current global order. Rather, we think that articulating these problems through 'social cohesion' obscures as much—or more—as it illuminates. Indeed, one of our central claims is that this term is frequently used in a way that assumes broad understanding, while in practice it is subject to competing and contradictory definitions and loaded with various implicit and explicit values. The book, then, is a critique of the *concept* of social cohesion, how it has developed and, more importantly, how it is *used*. We are not concerned with every possible approach to the question of how societies hold together—readers expecting a discussion of Durkheim, Weber, Parsons, or the broader sociological tradition would be disappointed. Indeed, as we discuss in chapter 1, it is common in the literature that we are criticizing to suggest that social cohesion is simply the most up to date form of one of the central concepts in sociology. This claim of continuity, however, misses how the term 'social cohesion' is in fact a relatively new arrival, whose usage has expanded exponentially in the past thirty to forty years. Our focus is on the nexus of social research, policy research, and policymaking within which this term has achieved and consolidated its position, and on some of the main ways in which this has proved problematic. We trace features of its development through the policy agendas of transnational and international bodies, and the reactions of social researchers to the demands of policymakers for a clear and usable concept, which is then reapplied in policy development and utilized as part of various development programs. In the course of its trajectory, the notion has attracted the attention of large numbers of public and private institutions and NGOs, who have put considerable resources into social cohesion research.

In the process, we argue, the term has undergone a substantial *thickening*, increasingly linked to substantive values (albeit in unclear and sometimes contradictory ways) and come increasingly to be represented as something that can be measured according to a single scale and thought of very much as a single substance that can be simply generated through policy interventions. As a result, social cohesion is increasingly taken for granted as a desirable feature of societies and a worthwhile policy goal, and as something whose meaning is stable and uncontroversial. The concept becomes masked behind a veneer of scientific authority and normative legitimacy, while beneath that veneer quite different, even contradictory, policies are grouped together. In part, then, we criticize social cohesion for its vagueness and its elevation into a kind of buzzword for discussing social policies that confuses more than it clarifies. However, our argument goes beyond that to suggest that the dominant framings of social cohesion discourse tend to reflect and stabilize aspects of the *status quo* and shield them from deeper criticism. The more that social cohesion is treated as a single substance with a clear and uncontroversial meaning, the more it narrows the space for debate and contestation around both the policies adopted in its name and the understanding of the social on which it rests. In contrast, we argue, social cohesion, if it is to mean anything, ought to be understood explicitly as a contested concept, and actively subject to contestation.

That is not to say that, throughout the development of this discourse, there has not been a more critical undercurrent (and one on which we draw and build in our critique).[5] However, the more common response of the literature we approach is simply to note these criticisms as an aspect of the challenges of defining and grasping the idea of social cohesion, before proceeding to get on with the task of offering a better definition or description of their own. In contrast, we do not want to offer our own, competing, definition to add to the noise, but rather, to examine the tensions, limitations, and contradictions within these definitions and their applications in order to think about what the concept is *doing*. In this sense, we are approaching 'social cohesion' in the spirit of critical theory, which aims to reveal how certain concepts are rooted in and limited by aspects of our current social and economic reality and reflect the interests and biases of certain institutions. In adopting this critical posture, we do not of course claim to be offering a value-free analysis. While we often point to contradictions within this literature, and to various ways in which it might fail to live up to its own promise, our goal is not to develop *only* an immanent critique. Our critique is also motivated by our own values, which will become clearer as the book develops—most obviously in chapter 5.

In focusing on this particular nexus, our criticism is entirely at the level of discourse. Although we draw on the work of others who have done so, we do not ourselves offer detailed critiques of the success or failure of these policies, in part because we do not want to assert our own criteria about what a good 'social cohesion' policy might achieve. Nor have we done the kind of field work that would make it possible to draw clear causal links between the various approaches, concepts, institutions, and interests that we identify. Moreover, such a focus might well open us to accusations of parochialism and irrelevance: if social cohesion is only a term of art in a narrow policy set, why dedicate such critical energy to it?

More troublingly, some have suggested that social cohesion's heyday in policy literature has largely passed. When discussing the theme of this book, for instance, one of us was told that it sounded "very 1990s." We have two responses to this. The first is that, as we demonstrate in detail in chapters 3 and 4, while social cohesion's prominence has waxed and waned, it appears to be undergoing a significant comeback in the aftermath of the COVID-19 pandemic. It has also, as chapter 4 discusses, moved beyond some of the contexts of its original formulation to influence international development practices. Even if these usages of the term might represent new developments that revise previous usages, it is important to attend to the way that they remain marked by them. Second, even if 'social cohesion' were to drop out of fashion, the kind of critique we offer here might also be applied to similar concepts.

Our critical approach also allows us to focus on a striking contradiction. The ubiquity of 'social cohesion' coincides with a consolidation of ways of thinking about economy and society that tend to downplay the significance of 'the social.'[6] The very things that studies of social cohesion are concerned with—particularly the *quality* of social relationships and issues of solidarity between and among social groups—are often seen as secondary, or even irrelevant. Margaret Thatcher's totemic insistence that there is no such thing as society, only individuals and families, for example, presented a world in which social issues were transformed into matters of individual morality or economic prosperity. In this context much contemporary literature on social cohesion looks like a belated recognition that these things in fact *do matter*, a 'rediscovery of the social.' Yet at the same time, the attempt to grasp this problem is limited by the very same frameworks that previously denied it was a problem. This orientation reduces the complexity of human relationships to single measures of value, seeing both complex relational goods as a single kind of thing, and economic growth as an undisputed good, the only proper measure of a society's success or failure. The result, we argue, is that one specific way of understanding and regulating how societies hold together becomes elevated to a general theory of human behavior and a 'one size fits all' policy approach. Indeed, the very drive to turn social cohesion into a matter of policy tends to exacerbate this, demanding easily packaged proposals that can be operationalized by public institutions.

As authors, we are also actors in the scenario we are criticizing. This book emerged from a research grant project concerning the concept of social cohesion. This term was chosen to reflect what we felt brought participants in the project together: an interest in co-operation, solidarity, mutual aid, social movements, care, and social ontology. It was a convenient badge for work which we felt, while diverse, shared some key themes. It was also, however, something that we thought would make our research more contemporary, relevant and 'problem-oriented.' Who, after all, could dispute that social cohesion is important and worth spending time researching? Had not successive waves of crisis shown that social cohesion was beginning to fray?

Evidently, the funders agreed. At that stage, we were largely unaware of the particular discourses and usages that we criticize: it was only once we began to develop the project that we discovered this peculiarly technical usage of 'social cohesion,' one that somehow manages to be too vague and too precise at the same time. While we never proposed to address policy solutions, we were clearly claiming some of social cohesion's aura to give legitimacy to our research, and this led us in turn to look more closely at how this concept was being used.

The book is structured as follows. Chapter 1 introduces the key trends and distinctions in the literature on social cohesion. It notes a general trend towards 'thick' concepts of social cohesion, which stretches the concept beyond its narrower, more 'everyday' meanings, and incorporates various constitutive elements and/or value concepts. It argues that, despite claims to the contrary, this is not a natural continuation of an older sociological literature, but a particular way of framing the social, characterized in particular by an emphasis on decline and threat and assumptions of 'ontological realism,' in which social cohesion is treated as something that can be tracked, measured, and generated. We then introduce several important distinctions: between universalist and particularist approaches; concerning the place of values in defining and discussing social cohesion; and concerning the scope and scale at which social cohesion is seen to exist.

Chapter 2 builds on this analysis by focusing on three prominent theoretical accounts of social cohesion, two of which can be broadly described as universalist and one as particularist. We argue that universalist approaches tend to assume ontological realism either by explicitly trying to identify a transhistorical notion of social cohesion or by discussing a historically specific and normatively defined concept *as if* it were a real property that can be quantified, compared, and made commensurate across different cultural contexts and thus assigned causal efficacy. We also focus on the role of values in such accounts, arguing that they often either depend explicitly on substantive (and controversial) value concepts, or introduce them implicitly through dependence on concepts such as tolerance and pluralism—making the assumption that social cohesion *must* be desirable in itself. Moreover, such approaches are characterized by what we call 'normative overdetermination,' in which the different levels and sources of normativity of social cohesion become confused and intermingled, inflating its importance and allowing for significant slippages in its usage. On the other hand, particularist approaches—while avoiding the most egregious problems inherent in the universalist approach by recognizing social cohesion as manifested differently across different societies—raise the question of whether there is any value in discussing social cohesion at all. The more that particularism pushes towards a focus on specific contexts, the more, we argue, the value of 'social cohesion' as a distinctive concept begins to dissolve.

Chapters 3 and 4 turn to the policy literature. Chapter 3 presents a detailed account of the evolution of the term 'social cohesion' from 1990 to 2022 in the two major supranational bodies in Europe: the European Union and the Council of Europe. Despite both bodies identifying social cohesion as a central concern of policy—as something that is under threat and that needs to be addressed—they link it to quite different policy agendas. The European Union consistently sees the value of social cohesion as linked to the needs of economic growth and competitiveness. The main threat to social cohesion is people 'falling behind' in a modernizing and technologizing world, and the solution is to integrate them into the economy through employment and training. The Council of Europe shares an emphasis on social exclusion as the main threat (or antonym) of social cohesion, but suggests a much broader picture of inclusion, based on the extension of social rights and civic participation. These examples thus demonstrate both the elasticity of social cohesion as a concept and also some of its underlying ideological presuppositions.

Chapter 4 looks at social cohesion's migration into the global arena through its use in international development, again by analyzing the shifting policy approaches of two major international bodies, the OECD and the UN. While these reflect some of the same problems identified in chapter 3, the context of international development adds an additional dimension to the analysis. The migration of 'social cohesion' into international development solidifies a sense that it is an ideal or goal towards which societies should work, dovetailing smoothly with development agendas—ones that have been criticized for imposing restrictive models of social development on diverse societies. A sincere desire to adapt social cohesion agendas to local conditions and secure legitimacy among local stakeholders sits uneasily alongside a desire to provide clear and comparable measures that allow for meaningful comparison and a push for a 'depoliticized' concept that can be neutrally applied.

Chapter 5 pulls together the critiques of the previous chapters, suggesting that the dominant framings of social cohesion make it harder to approach it critically and tend to reflect and stabilize the contexts in which they emerge. Despite their sometimes-critical intent, these framings take for granted elements of the *status quo* and thus shield them from deeper criticism. While we argue that this should give us pause about 'social cohesion' *at all*, we suggest that it might be too late, or perhaps even unwise, to abandon it entirely. Instead, we suggest some ways that it might be opened to contestation, allowing it to be criticized more openly and used more critically.

Thus, we hope that this book will be of interest to people in a range of fields. The book is short, and we hope that readers will approach it as a whole. Nonetheless, those interested in social and political science might gain the most from chapters 1 and 2. For social and political philosophers, it should be read as a call to approach social cohesion critically and not to simply import its use from social science disciplines. For social scientists and researchers, we provide a challenge to the idea that social cohesion ought to be approached as a single, measurable substance tracked across different contexts. Those interested in policy and international relations will gain more from chapters 3 and 4, which both provide a narrative of how the concept has developed and transformed and offer some trenchant criticisms. Chapter 5, we hope, will be of interest to anyone who has had to encounter and engage with the concept of social cohesion 'in the wild' and had to think about how to either criticize it or shape their own interests and agendas within it—whether they are scholars, politicians, civil servants, students, social movement or community activists, or just plain members of the public.

The book is a call to open 'social cohesion' to contestation, debate, and democratic ownership and to push it in a direction that would allow it to play a constructive part in offering a deeper critique of our present.

Chapter 1

Staking Out the Terrain

Key Trends and Distinctions in Social Cohesion

On Boxing Day 1948, Bertrand Russell delivered the first BBC Reith Lecture. The series of six lectures was entitled *Authority and the Individual*, and the first lecture was entitled 'Social Cohesion and Human Nature.' In it, Russell poses the question "how can we combine that degree of individual initiative which is necessary for progress with the degree of social cohesion that is necessary for survival?"[1] Social cohesion is here contrasted with "the other side of the life of man in communities, namely individual initiative."[2] In Russell's treatment, "Social cohesion, which started with loyalty to a group reinforced by the fear of enemies, grew by processes partly natural and partly deliberate until it reached the vast conglomerations that we now know as nations."[3] In history, this cohesion might be driven either by personal loyalty, tribal loyalty, or fear ("Sparta was praised throughout antiquity for its admirable social cohesion, but it was a cohesion which never attempted to embrace the whole population, except in so far as terror compelled outward loyalty"[4]), and, at a certain stage of development, "a loyalty based not on territorial affinity or similarity of race, but on the identity of creed."[5] Central to cohesion in Russell's account is not only fear of a centralized authority, but also fear of outsiders: "Always when we pass beyond the limits of the family it is the external enemy which supplies the cohesive force."[6] Indeed, this is Russell's problem: How, in an era of nuclear weapons, when all rational arguments suggest the need for global harmony, can we reconcile this with the apparent fact that "a world state, if it were firmly established, would have no enemies to fear and would therefore be in danger of breaking down through a lack of cohesive force."[7]

Russell's problem is not our problem, and it would take us too far from our main focus to examine him further. Nonetheless, it is striking to hear these lectures seventy-five years later, and to hear what a *thin* conception of social cohesion they depend on. Russell's social cohesion can have many sources, including notably fear of both centralized authority and outsiders. Its degree varies, but it is measured only in terms of intensity of social bonds (and ultimately whether a society holds together or collapses). It is in contrast with elements of individual initiative and genius, and while compatible with a degree of individual liberty it does not depend on it and is often threatened by it. Compare this with the entry by Manca in the *Encyclopedia of Quality of Life and Well-Being Research*, which was the first description of social cohesion offered by a cursory Google search early in this project:

> Social cohesion is a social process which aims to consolidate plurality of citizenship by reducing inequality and socioeconomic disparities and fractures in the society. It reflects people's needs for both personal development and a sense of belonging and links together individual freedom and social justice, economic efficiency and the fair sharing of resources, and pluralism and common rules for resolving all conflicts.[8]

If Russell's understanding of social cohesion is thin, then Manca's is *thick*, both in the sense that it builds into social cohesion several constitutive elements beyond simply the fact of holding together, and that it invokes substantive normative values (and rather a lot of them).[9] Sparta, for example, would evidently not have been socially cohesive on this definition.

1.1 THE THICKENING OF SOCIAL COHESION

Manca's definition is perhaps one of the thickest, but it is far from unusual in this respect. Contemporary approaches to social cohesion often go far beyond the simple fact of holding together. Social cohesion appears to have moved from a basic description of the various ways in which societies hold together to something far more specific: a kind of substance or essence that societies can have more or less of, that can be tracked and measured, that is embedded in specific institutional arrangements, linked to specific values, and made the object of active policy interventions. At the same time, while never severed from it completely, it appears increasingly distant from the everyday meaning of 'holding together.' This 'thickening' of the term has gone hand in hand with an explosion in its usage—an increase which begins in the 1990s and continues to rise today.[10] One important aspect of this 'thickening' is social cohesion's increasing emergence as a distinct policy goal and the accompanying assumption that it describes a good or desirable feature of society, linked in particular to concepts such as well-being and quality of life. Its use as a term for describing social reality increasingly becomes conflated and combined with these normative levels of analysis.

It is this 'thickened' discourse on social cohesion that we are concerned with. We suggest that this needs to be approached as a relatively new development, part of the rapid rise of 'social cohesion' as a specific concept. It is true that questions of social order, stability and how society 'holds together' have regularly appeared in political philosophy and social theory, often as central structuring concerns in the work of Hobbes, Tocqueville, Durkheim, and so forth. Contemporary treatments of social cohesion in both policy and social research frequently draw on this intellectual lineage to frame social cohesion as one of the central questions of sociology. Dragolov et al., for example, identify it as far back as Ibn Kaldun's *Muqaddimah*,[11] while Durkheim's *The Division of Labour in Society* is most frequently cited as the classical source for the concept.[12] In this framing, social cohesion is simply the latest (most advanced, scientific) name for an age-old problem. However, these engagements with classical sociology rarely go beyond a passing first footnote, and often assume that 'social cohesion' can be uncomplicatedly identified with other terms.[13] For example, the term *cohésion sociale* and its cognates appear only marginally in Durkheim's work, the central concern of which is solidarity (*solidarité*).[14] There is a risk, then, that tracing an unbroken lineage between such concepts misses the specificity of both. In a striking example of this, Dragolov et al. suggest that in the famous French revolutionary motto of "*liberté, égalité, fraternité*," the "latter goal . . . seems to be the call of the French Revolution for a cohesive society" which, in contrast to the first two "in its modern guise of social cohesion has only recently begun to gain prominence as a core good to be sustained by political action and civil society."[15] This is only coherent if either the concept of fraternity is denuded of all of its more complex meanings (e.g., of solidarity and brotherhood), or social cohesion is inflated to include them. Moreover, it avoids the question of why, if social cohesion is a perennial question of sociology, the term 'social cohesion' undergoes such a substantial growth in usage over the past thirty years.

We thus approach 'social cohesion' not as simply a more modern-sounding version of something much older, but at the same time as part of a historically specific way of representing the social that serves contemporary ends. As Dobbernack puts it, "Efforts to define and especially to quantify cohesion do not mirror social realities that are unproblematically legible and, despite any claim to the contrary, are neither neutral nor natural."[16] Like all concepts developed by social sciences, social cohesion both frames social and political problems and concerns and helps make the social legible to policymakers. As such, it also excludes things from its frame and leaves other elements illegible—it does not merely help us grasp a pre-given social realm but constitutes and determines how we think about that realm. In particular, contemporary accounts of social cohesion are shaped by two implicit ideas. The first is an idea of decline or threat.[17] The fear that social cohesion is in some way in decline or under threat forms the underlying assumption of the discourse with which we are concerned. This threat may take many different forms: globalization, multiculturalism, inequality, unemployment, deindustrialization, an overweening welfare state, competitive individualism, democratic deficit, and so on. While this concern frames social research, it is even more prominent for politicians for whom social cohesion discourse is almost always a response to fears of social cohesion fraying and declining.[18] It is not hard to see why this is. Narratives of decline and restoration are rhetorically extremely powerful. The decline thesis provides politicians a way to link various social ills and grievances into a clear narrative, to put a name to a sense of crisis and to frame desired policies as responses to it.

As we will develop in chapters 3 and 4, 'social cohesion' begins to acquire prominence in policy discourses in the early 1990s, responding to perceived threats of dissolution brought about by 'economic modernization' and the apparent failures of the welfare state. This was a context in which 'big ideas' and 'visions' about the good life were increasingly seen as suspect, linked on the one hand to an idea of the end of history and on the other to liberal commitments to pluralism. In this context, Dobbernack suggests that social cohesion played a particularly useful role in framing problems and solutions.[19] Politicians from many different political traditions can agree on the need for social cohesion, while at the same time taking advantage of its ideological capaciousness and elasticity to frame their own agendas within it: "It is sometimes deployed in rightwing and populist politics by those who long for the good old days when life seemed easier, safer and less threatening. But social cohesion can also be used by those who fear the consequences of excessively marketised visions of the future."[20] This is accompanied by a sense of novelty: "Old ways of regulating society, of conceiving of social solidarity, social assistance, crime or urban unrest, are contrasted with novel approaches that purport to make use of resources of social solidarity that had previously been ignored or stifled."[21] At the same time, solutions to the problems of social cohesion seem to present themselves as readily available, even sometimes through the very same things presented as threats (for example, we discuss in chapter 4 the OECD's sense that economic flexibility and reform is both a threat *and* "a motor of the economic growth and prosperity on which cohesion can thrive").[22] Social cohesion discourse is thus frequently based on a "characteristic coincidence of lack and fullness" that often accompanies this emphasis on decline and disintegration.[23] Social cohesion is in decline or at risk, but the capacity to restore it always lies latently just below the surface. Again, this is particularly attractive for politicians, both because it invokes a vision of restoration in which the whole of society might once more come together, and because it articulates a particular position for policymakers within that. Latent potentials for cohesiveness can be activated if only the right policy mixture is applied and people are provided the right kind of incentives and nudges.

Underscoring the fear of decline is a second assumption, which Gregersen calls 'ontological realism'—social cohesion exists "as a distinct entity upon which agents may act and [which in turn] influences the workings of sociality."[24] This appears to follow smoothly (though not inevitably) from the decline thesis, insofar as it implies something that can go up and down, strengthen or weaken, or be created through the right kinds of activity and interventions. This is evident in the multiplicity of metaphors of substance in this discourse: social cohesion is the glue that holds society together, or a social cement. Another prominent example of this is the Social Cohesion Radar developed by Dragolov et al., which we discuss in more detail in chapter 2. The metaphor of a radar, which detects something that is there but we cannot see through other means, captures perfectly the approach this entails.[25]

The two assumptions (decline and ontological realism) are independent of each other: it is possible to believe social cohesion is under threat without treating it as a distinct entity or substance, and it is possible to treat social cohesion as a distinct entity or substance without believing it is in decline. Indeed, ontological realism is often employed *against* the decline thesis in those studies that take it seriously. A Eurofound report (using the same approach as Dragolov et al.) failed to find evidence that social cohesion was in decline (or indeed that it was not).[26] Yet in practice, the decline thesis often persists. For example, a recent literature review of social cohesion, noted that the Eurofound report provides "reasons for optimism alongside the obvious fracture points."[27] The obviousness of the fracture points apparently remains even while empirical evidence to the contrary is accepted. This indicates precisely how we see the two theses interacting to shape this discourse: Politicians invoke decline and pose their policies in terms of restoration; social research either serves this agenda by considering which policies best enhance cohesion or challenge it by looking for evidence that it is not in decline. Either way, they look for an operationalizable concept of social cohesion that can be measured, which in turn reinforces the idea that social cohesion is, whether in decline or not, something we should be concerned with. Thus, a recent article proposing to measure social cohesion in Korea both cites the OECD as authority for the claim that "the demand for action is even bigger for South Korea as the country is going through continual demise of social cohesion" and at the same time *asserts* "it has to be admitted that we don't have an agreed measurement of the concept that can consistently gauge each country's position on social cohesion because even defining social cohesion presents lots of trouble for researchers."[28]

In the following chapters we will develop some aspects of this picture in more detail, but for the remainder of this chapter we will sketch out some of the conceptual terrain that shapes approaches to social cohesion in order to better orient some of our criticisms. While these more conceptual considerations skew more heavily towards the social research side of the equation, they also provide a framework to reflect on the use of the concept overall.

1.2 UNIVERSALIST AND PARTICULARIST

As we have seen, discussing social cohesion tends naturally to raise the question of what it *is*. In this section, we distinguish two broad categories of approach to this question, but before we do so, it is worth pausing to discuss the question of definition. A common approach to social cohesion assumes it is necessary to *define* the concept before using it. As we will see in later chapters, this is connected to the desire to quantify, measure, and operationalize it in order to judge the effectiveness of policy interventions. Yet philosophers are, or should be, well aware of the problem of approaching real-world phenomena in terms of strict definition.[29] If definition is understood in terms of the requirement to give necessary and sufficient conditions, then this often fails to capture the genuine complexity of concepts. Indeed, it is hard to even grasp what it would mean to provide such conditions for 'social cohesion'—what does it mean to say x is an instance of social cohesion if (and only if) it meets conditions y and z? It might be possible to give necessary and sufficient conditions for something like a 'socially cohesive society,' but it is striking that this is not how these accounts tend to proceed: Rather, they take themselves to be defining a particular kind of *thing*. Similarly, if Nietzsche is correct that "only that which has no history is definable,"[30] then the assumption that social cohesion is in need of definition risks dehistoricizing and universalizing the concept in ways that are misleading. For our purposes, it is worth stressing we do not see the solution to any of the problems we identify in terms of giving a better or worse definition, and indeed suspect that the search for definition is part of the problem. To the extent that we use the language of definition in what follows we are simply engaging with these approaches on their own terms, without endorsing either the possibility or desirability of definition itself.

Answers to the question of what kind of thing social cohesion is vary quite widely. In Manca's definition cited above, it is described as a "process";[31] but Chan et al. explicitly reject this, arguing that it implies an "end state" or "maximal level" of social cohesion, and insisting instead that it must be a "state of affairs."[32] Dragolov et al. suggest social cohesion concerns the "quality of social cooperation,"[33] while Aruqaj suggests it ought to be seen as a "social fact"[34] involving people's "propensity" to "cooperate with each other as members of society, across key cleavages, and with institutions."[35] As we will see in the following sections and chapters, social cohesion also begins to take on a sense of ideal or goal, often approximating some kind of idea of good society, particularly in some of the policy literature that we will discuss in chapters 3 and 4. While each of these bring with them some fairly weighty ontological presuppositions, there is relatively little sustained reflection on their significance.

Nonetheless, we can usefully note that many approaches to social cohesion treat it as a unitary thing that can be tracked and compared across societies. In this view social cohesion is *the* process, property, quality, or state of affairs to which we refer whenever we say that a society, community or group is cohesive. It is the *same* process, quality, or state of affairs that is manifested irrespective of the particular time, place or cultural context. Let us call this a *universalist* approach to social cohesion.[36] On this point of view, social cohesion is something which societies either have or do not (or have more or less of), and whether they have it or not can be identified on the presence or absence of certain constituent elements or dimensions. These elements depend on certain antecedents and have certain consequents. The elements, and perhaps even the antecedents, are socially invariable insofar as all socially cohesive societies possess them, and if a society does not possess them (or enough of them), it is not, whatever else might be said about it, socially cohesive.[37] One of the overarching goals of this book is to criticize and reject this approach to social cohesion. But before proceeding with this critique, it is worth highlighting some of its more peculiar aspects. First, as we noted with the example of Sparta, if social cohesion is specified to a reasonable degree of detail, then many societies will turn out not to be socially cohesive even if they might appear to 'cohere' perfectly well. Second, this approach implies it is not possible for any given phenomenon to be a dimension, component, or indicator of social cohesion in one society but be a threat to or irrelevant for social cohesion in another.

The alternative to a universalist approach to social cohesion might be called a *particularist* approach: On this basis, social cohesion refers to *any* property, quality, process, or state of affairs that we refer to when we describe a society as cohesive. Crucially, this might be different depending on the specific society, the historical and cultural context, and the time and place of the society. Thus, social cohesion might look radically different between societies, and its antecedents and consequents may similarly differ with respect to the time, place, and cultural context of its manifestation. This thus implies a 'thinner' definition of social cohesion, insofar as it does not build into the definition specific constitutive elements and recognizes various different societies as cohesive insofar as they 'hold together.' Nonetheless, for this to be described as *cohesion* at all it needs to be demonstrated that societies do *in fact* hold together—it should be possible then to point to certain features that ensure this, which might be shared across societies that share relevant contexts. In this sense, we can say not that there is one single way in which social cohesion is manifest, but rather that it can be manifest in various different *regimes*. This is the approach favored by Green and Janmaat, for whom "social cohesion refers to the property by which whole societies, and the individuals within them, are bound together through the action of specific attitudes, behaviors, rules and institutions that rely on consensus rather than pure coercion."[38] We will discuss this approach in more detail in the next chapters, but at this stage it is worth noting that even these approaches go somewhat further than Russell, insofar as cohesion remains distinguished from bare coercion.

It is worth noting that the distinction between universalist and particularist approaches does not map perfectly on to the language of thick and thin that we have employed earlier. While particularist approaches are generally likely to be thinner, universalist approaches might be more or less thick depending on how they develop their specific definitions and components (the two examples we focus on in chapter 2 represent quite different approaches in this respect). Nonetheless, universalist accounts tend towards thickness because they are required to specify various components, elements, and dimensions of social cohesion as well as the indicators that might be used to measure and compare it across societies. The literature on social cohesion contains a wide array of components or dimensions, including "trust" (social and institutional), "openness" (or "acceptance of diversity"), "equality" (either of opportunities or wealth), "well-being," "shared values," and "shared identity."[39] These usually combine social relations, patterns of behavior, and social institutions, which might be broadly described as objective, with attitudes, beliefs, and values, which might be described as subjective.[40] However, many popular components *also* appear as indicators, conditions, or outcomes of social cohesion, meaning that one of the most common refrains in the literature on social cohesion is that these are too often specified in contradictory and conflicting ways.[41] Beyond the general confusion this causes at worst it can collapse into arguments by definition, in which, for example, the connection between equality and social cohesion is simply stipulated without serious investigation.[42] Thus, much of the literature, especially in the last decade, has sought to untangle and separate more clearly these various elements. For example: "Instead of falling into the temptation to combine all conceivable and desirable qualities of society under the label of cohesion, . . . cohesion can be measured and understood only if it is isolated from other social phenomena such as inequality, poverty, or life satisfaction."[43] It is easy to see here how such an approach tends towards ontological realism. If social cohesion is a single kind of thing, if it is something that can be measured and compared (if, indeed, enabling measurement and comparison is its purpose), then it makes sense to invoke metaphors of substances and detectable phenomena.

This confusion is sometimes attributed to social cohesion's use (or abuse) by policymakers, with social researchers stressing its emergence as a "panacea for the numerous new social cleavages" and the need for each individual agency to produce its own "problem-driven" concept.[44] It is certainly true, as we will see more in future chapters, that the various concepts developed by policy organizations tend to be more conflicted and confused, and that sometimes this diversity is even celebrated ("the broad scope of the term can have advantages, allowing a more flexible application and wider-ranging acceptance").[45] However, it would be wrong to assume that these problems can be somehow narrowly confined to policy literature. First, it is still possible to find these kinds of confusions repeated, for example, in passages like the following: "Lower social cohesion can result in negative social consequences. For instance, a high level of inequalities, a potential indicator of weaker social cohesion, can lead to higher crime rates, undermine public well-being and a sense of community, and disrupt the social fabric."[46]

Moreover, while universalist social research often seeks to distinguish itself from the confusions of policy literature, it also seeks to serve the ends of that policy by offering a measurable concept. The purpose of isolating social cohesion from other phenomena is precisely to "attend to the most pressing questions for social policy."[47] Thus, social cohesion is to be disentangled from the messy world of policy debates, *in order to be handed back in a more usable form*. In this way, as we will address in the next chapter, they are still shaped by the needs of the policy literature, and often draw with them some of its assumptions and presuppositions. In this context, it is notable that the desire on the part of social researchers for a more precise, measurable concept does not appear to have led to much convergence on a specific concept. While it is possible to demonstrate some shared themes across the literature, researchers still tend to come up with their own, new measurement through rejection and criticism of the old. While, of course, disagreement in the social sciences is normal, especially when it comes to defining social concepts, this becomes a problem insofar as the concept is designed to guide policy. More generally, this widespread disagreement might give us pause for thought regarding the usage of the concept: Perhaps it is not a concept that ought to be isolated and clarified in this way, but rather something like an essentially contested concept (we return to this point in chapter 5).

1.3 SOCIAL COHESION AND VALUES

Alongside the distinction between particularist and universalist conceptions of social cohesion, it is also useful to look at the role of normative values in accounts of social cohesion. It is common to find normative values of various kinds built into conceptions of social cohesion as either dimensions, components, or indicators. These include notions such as 'well-being,' 'equality,' 'freedom,' 'fair sharing of resources,' 'legitimacy,' and 'social justice.' We can call these approaches *substantive* insofar as they are committed to including specific values and normative principles into their definition of social cohesion. Once again, it is clear to see why these might be controversial: First, they tend to build into the concept ideas that go some way beyond the sense of holding together. Must societies promote equality to be cohesive? Can societies based on deep injustice not also hold together? Moreover (as mentioned above) in doing so they risk assuming by definition claims that are in fact in need of defense, that is, that more equal societies are also more cohesive or that greater levels of cohesion (however defined) lead to greater well-being.

The alternative to such approaches would be *formalist* approaches to social cohesion, which exclude particular values or normative principles, in favor of apparently more descriptive concepts such as 'participation,' 'belonging,' 'sharing,' and 'trust.' Of course, such concepts can be used in a normative fashion, and their application and use has normative implications, but, unlike those values used in the substantive definitions, they might plausibly be used in a non-normative fashion, and can be observed through more or less disinterested observation. At the same time, they clearly depend on individuals within society possessing and endorsing certain values themselves. Mirroring the discussion of subjective and objective elements above, it is helpful to distinguish (in at least some cases) from the objective manifestation of values and their subjective endorsement. For example, equality (at least of income and wealth) might be manifested without being endorsed as particularly important (some accounts suggest this is a feature of Japanese society). Similarly, Dragolov et al. argue that social cohesion can be measured using *perceptions* of unfairness but not *objective manifestations* of it. Thus a socially cohesive society can be an unfair one, but not one its citizens perceive as unfair. Likewise, they exclude diversity from social cohesion but stress that "in modern societies, social cohesion is only possible if people are able to deal appropriately with diversity—this is why we include acceptance of diversity as one crucial dimension."[48] Thus subjective attitudes towards and beliefs about values form a component of social cohesion even when values themselves do not.

One extremely common approach to this issue is to emphasize the importance of *shared* values as a component of social cohesion.[49] Holtug notes an important ambivalence in this idea, however: is it the sharing that matters, or the specific values themselves? He argues, "It is implausible to claim that sharing a particular set of values promotes social cohesion, no matter what that set consists in."[50] Sharing some values ("tolerance, beneficence, equality, optimism, dialogue, and faith in democracy") will likely support social cohesion, but "sharing an identity based on intolerance, short-term egoism, pessimism, inequality and lack of faith in dialogue and democracy seems unlikely to do so."[51] This, he argues, is for both conceptual and empirical reasons. First, these values conceptually rule out certain aspects of social cohesion, especially solidarity (understood in terms of "favouring redistribution to the advantage of those who are worse off than you are").[52] Second, the adoption of these values will have detrimental consequences for social cohesion itself, "for example, intolerance and short-term egoism would seem to make people rather unreliable and untrustworthy."[53]

It is evident here that Holtug sees solidarity and trust as definitional components of social cohesion (in part because he identifies it with social capital, something far from consistent across the literature, as we discuss further below). But if we do not make that equation, then the thesis he rejects seems much less implausible. Indeed, is it really so difficult to imagine a society based on intolerance and short-term egoism holding together over a sustained period of time? Might a lack of faith in dialogue and democracy in fact be rather conducive to a society holding together if it meant a lack of dissent and public disagreement? The assumption that the specific values matter more than the fact they are shared seems to assume a thick conception of social cohesion, but a thinner approach based on simply holding together might emphasize that sharing is more important than the specific values. Moreover, emphasizing values such as tolerance and faith in democracy (note *faith in*, rather than the existence of actual democratic institutions) seems to tie social cohesion strongly to a particular context of diverse, liberal democratic societies. This raises questions about its plausibility as a general concept (especially, as we discuss in chapter 4, when it becomes applied as part of development programs across the globe).

This discussion points to a further complication in the role of values in social cohesion generated by the prominence of concepts such as pluralism, openness, and tolerance. Some accounts reject the necessity for shared values while at the same time suggesting that social cohesion is based on an "acceptance of diversity"[54] or a minimal "normative consensus" around "shared norms that are essential to collective togetherness, and that do not negate individual and group differences altogether."[55] Yet these remain values of some kind, albeit of a 'second-order' kind. Such second-order values are common in social cohesion accounts (reflecting an underlying assumption that cohesion must be compatible with—if not unique to—liberal democratic societies). According to Broadhead, "Any discussion of social cohesion with an equalities approach cannot be based on a homogenous sense of a society. It needs to acknowledge the plurality of that society, as well as the inequalities it contains."[56] Thus social cohesion implies both the fact of pluralism/plurality and a subjective commitment to pluralism on the part of citizens. While this might appear to be a more open and flexible account of social cohesion than one that relies on cultural similarity or the endorsement of substantive values, it still presents quite a demanding picture, insofar as it demands that subjectively held values are in some sense compatible with pluralism, and elevates certain values (tolerance, diversity) above others. As we will discuss in future chapters, this remains compatible with various forms of exclusion, and can also serve to obscure deeper disagreement about substantive values, especially when these concepts are wielded by politicians for their own ends.

In addition to shared values, some accounts of social cohesion draw on somewhat looser ideas of a shared project or endeavor. Examples include "a pronounced focus on the common good,"[57] "generally enabling people to have a sense they are engaged in a common enterprise,"[58] "a sense of mutual commitment,"[59] and "common aims and objectives."[60] As with 'second-order' values like tolerance and pluralism, these might be seen as an alternative to shared values in the strong sense, but there are important ambivalences here, especially when it comes to how these notions of common good or enterprise are understood—is it, for example, reducible to the goods of individual members of society, or is it something that exists over and above them (we return to this point in chapter 5)? Does having common aims and objectives simply involve wanting the same things ('everyone wants to be a millionaire') or does it require a complementary and cooperatively achieved objective? Moreover, these ideas risk their own exclusions, especially insofar as society is represented as a team all pulling together in the same direction. One report by Eurofound asserts, "Social scientists are convinced that, in societies as in sports teams, cohesion represents a positive quality that brings with it a sense of resilience and a marked orientation towards the common good."[61] This can obscure real tensions and antagonisms within society by assuming that they can be overcome by simply aligning or changing attitudes and behaviors. If the team is not performing it is the coach's job to remind everyone they are all in it together and exhort them to pull themselves together.

So far, we have focused on the role of values within conceptions of social cohesion, though a similar, but importantly distinct, question can be raised concerning whether social cohesion *itself* is of normative value. Certainly, those accounts that build various normative values into social cohesion might be more likely to argue that social cohesion is good, but even those that rely on a purely formalist account might nonetheless agree that social cohesion is itself a good thing; policymakers would not be concerned with promoting social cohesion if they did not believe it was valuable in some sense. Thus, it is useful to distinguish between *normative* accounts of social cohesion, in which social cohesion is represented as itself normatively valuable, and *non-normative accounts* of social cohesion, which limit it to a purely descriptive phenomenon. Strictly speaking, of course, normative treatments of social cohesion might represent it is a *bad* thing—perhaps insofar as it holds back individual initiative or holds together bad societies—but more commonly normative accounts represent it as a good thing. The most substantive normative accounts are those we mentioned above in which social cohesion begins to approach a regulative ideal or a vision of good society. Such accounts present obvious risks insofar as various values can be wrapped up in a social cohesion program without substantive argument. As Gregersen notes, "This problem stems from the observation that the meaning of 'SC' approximates 'good society' in the political discourse. Justifications for cohesion policies thus resemble tautologies: One should promote a good society because it is good. Correspondingly, policies contrary to SC are predefined as bad."[62]

However, just as important is the question of *why* social cohesion is valuable: is it of *intrinsic* value or does it possess *instrumental* value as a means to other goods? For example, Holtug sees social cohesion (and its associated values of solidarity and trust) as instrumentally valuable for ensuring an egalitarian and free society, suggesting that of the classical revolutionary triad of *egalité*, *liberté*, and *fraternité*, the third may be "less basic" (though not as a result unimportant).[63] Many accounts stress that social cohesion ought to be seen as instrumentally valuable for well-being and happiness,[64] while others stress more prosaic concerns of the state, such as political stability, economic growth, and saving public money by reducing the need for social benefits or the provision of public services.[65] At the same time, as we will illustrate further in the following chapters, social cohesion is often *implicitly* treated as of intrinsic value, seen as a good to be balanced against others, or allowing its desirability as a concept to dictate the inclusion or exclusion of certain components or dimensions.

It is worth pausing on the idea of a non-normative account of social cohesion. From a social scientific point of view, such a perspective makes sense—if the goal is to simply descriptively analyze a phenomenon, then a non-normative approach is coherent and methodologically appropriate (it might even be appropriate to combine this with a substantive approach, as long as those values that are contained within social cohesion are not explicitly endorsed). On the other hand, there is a faint sense of paradox about the idea of a non-normative approach in policy. Even if social cohesion simply neutrally describes the capacity by which societies continue to hold together, then it might be argued that states (and thus governments and policy makers) have an interest in it and thus a reason to pursue it (though a revolutionary government might have reason to oppose it, or at least to oppose one form of it to another). Similarly, though more controversially, it might be argued that members of society also have a minimal interest in their society holding together, both because they value that society, and because social stability is a necessary condition for them to pursue other goods (though again, it is perfectly possible to imagine societies containing large numbers of people who would benefit more from its dissolution).

We can thus identify several levels on which social cohesion might be seen as normatively valuable: as an intrinsic good of some kind, perhaps containing certain substantive values; as instrumentally valuable for other goods; as something that states have a minimal interest in. The interaction of these different levels can give rise to various conceptual slippages. Is equality good because it helps social cohesion, is social cohesion good because it provides the basis for equality, or is social cohesion good because it also *means* equality and equality is also good? Does social cohesion permit pluralism or is pluralism an element of social cohesion? If certain values are built into the idea of social cohesion, then it might seem unnecessary to specify what other goods social cohesion is a means for. More significantly, the bare fact that states/societies have an interest, *ceteris paribus*, in continuing to exist can also become conflated with more specific and substantive values that it might otherwise be in conflict or have no necessary relationship with. There is no doubt that this can be useful: "By blurring the end of political actions, the elasticity of SC arguments makes it hard to hold policymakers accountable."[66] Once again, then, it seems that social cohesion risks becoming a cipher for discussing more substantive social issues, one which ultimately obscures the specific normative disagreements that might be involved by invoking something that is hard, if not impossible, to disagree with.

1.4 SCOPE AND SCALE OF SOCIAL COHESION

A final crucial question raised by discussions of social cohesion is the level of group, society, or community that is expected to be cohesive. Firstly, accounts of social cohesion vary about whether social cohesion is a property of society as a whole or a property of groups within society. Social cohesion is frequently discussed alongside the concept of social capital, which often accompanies Durkheim's treatment of solidarity in being presented as a precursor to social cohesion.[67] The two concepts gained popularity during the same period and under the same conditions,[68] and as a result social capital is often identified with or seen as a proxy for or indicator of social cohesion.

However, the most recent literature on social cohesion tends to distinguish them precisely by the appropriate scope and scale at which they are applied. Social capital is generally represented as a property of individuals and/or small-scale communities. In his famous popularization of the concept, Robert Putnam identified two forms of social capital, 'bonding capital'—which binds together individuals in close knit groups; and 'bridging capital'—which allows linking between these groups.[69] Crucially, as the metaphor of 'capital' implied, these remained a kind of individual possession, which societies may have more or less of *in aggregate*, but which were not possessed by society as a whole. In contrast, most accounts of social cohesion stress that it makes no sense to see an individual as 'cohesive,' and instead see social cohesion operating at a higher level, most commonly that of the society as a whole.[70] Thus, Dragolov et al. argue, "While social capital captures the individual's access to resources through social networks, social cohesion is concerned with a social entity as a whole."[71] Similarly, Green and Janmaat argue, citing the example of Northern Ireland and the combination of strong ties *within* Unionist and Republican communities with low cohesion *between* them, that a "country may well be rich in social capital, in terms of the social capital that resides in different groups, but this will not necessarily make it a cohesive society."[72]

The example of Northern Ireland (described as a 'country' within the UK context but one with an extremely contested history and not a sovereign state) indicates a second issue with the scope of social cohesion: Any account of social cohesion that attempts to apply it to a whole *society* requires an appropriate definition of society—inevitably, the most common understanding of society here is something coextensive with the nation or the territorial limits of the state. This is understandable, especially when what is desired is an operationalizable policy concept: the state is the level at which policy is made, at which institutions operate, and at which citizenship and the bounds of political participation are defined.[73] In this sense, Green and Janmaat see this assumption as part of a "necessary ground-clearing" to help identify the forms of cohesion in "actual societies." However, this ground-clearing plays a role in shaping the field of discussion in ways that it would be a mistake to lose sight of. This is particularly important, since many accounts of social cohesion stress not only the 'horizontal' relationships among groups, but also the 'vertical' relationships between citizens and various public and state institutions (expressed or indicated through, e.g., active participation or institutional trust). Defining the relevant unit of social cohesion as the existing nation state risks hypostatizing or taking for granted the existing structure of those states, and also potentially loses sight of other social relationships that transcend or cross the borders of existing states. It also assumes that the limits of 'society' are in some sense coextensive with state borders, which raises some quite complex questions of who counts as 'part of' a society at any given time. Compare, for example, one of the authors of this book, a foreigner with permanent residence in an EU state, with South Asian workers building World Cup stadiums in Qatar—which of us, if any, contribute to social cohesion of the societies in which we live?

At its worst, we might criticize this as a prime example of the *methodological nationalism* that has increasingly been identified as a problem in contemporary political and social theory.[74] In their influential account, Andreas Wimmer and Nina Glick Schiller identify three ways in which this methodological nationalism manifests itself:

> 1) ignoring or disregarding the fundamental importance of nationalism for modern societies; this is often combined with 2) naturalization, i.e., taking for granted that the boundaries of the nation-state delimit and define the unit of analysis; 3) territorial limitation which confines the study of social processes to the political and geographic boundaries of a particular nation-state.[75]

The second and third of these features are most evident in the social cohesion literature. This is partially due to desires for simplification and ground clearing of the sort defended by Green and Janmaat, but it is also clearly influenced by social cohesion's connection to policy and national politics. Wimmer and Glick Schiller argue that the tendency for naturalization gains its force partially from "the compartmentalization of the social science project into different 'national' academic fields, a process strongly influenced not only by nationalist thinking itself, but also by the institutions of the nation-state organizing and channeling social science thinking in universities, research institutions and government think tanks."[76] While in the following chapters we will analyze policy developments at the international and supranational level, we will see repeatedly how the national unit is assumed to be the main locus for measuring and tracking social cohesion, and the appropriate level for applying policies and programs.

It is also possible, though less evident, to identify the first element of methodological nationalism in the social cohesion discourse, in which "the prevalence of the nation-state model as the universal form of political organization are neither problematized nor made objects of study in their own right."[77] It is notable that the focus on shared values and goals often avoids mentioning specific ideas of the nation, preferring to talk broadly in terms of "mutual commitment,"[78] "common aims and objectives,"[79] "a sense of belonging,"[80] or "a pronounced focus on the common good."[81] Nationalism (of whatever form) is often not mentioned directly at all, despite the fact that articulations of shared values will often be defined and understood in national terms. Indeed, politicians themselves are rarely shy about this (especially in the context of immigration), happy to identify certain values as necessarily

British or intimately connected to French Republicanism. In this context, methodological nationalism does not only take for granted the existence of the nation as the appropriate unit for analysis, it also means that "even the most sophisticated theorizing about the modern condition accepted as a given that nationalist forms of inclusion and exclusion bind modern societies together."[82]

Not all accounts of social cohesion identify society with nation. Among the broad literature, social cohesion is approached at a number of different levels. For example, some accounts, propose that the most appropriate unit for social cohesion is the city, as both the site of most people's day-to-day experiences of social interaction and the site of major challenges to cohesion, most notably urban riots (which are of course cited as evidence of the decline thesis).[83] Others look at an even smaller scale, to specific neighborhoods and communities. While in the coming chapters we focus largely on accounts that identify society with nation, these mid- and small-scale analyses should not be ignored, and in some respects may present a useful alternative to the trends we criticize by allowing closer attention to, for example, social interactions across borders or more localized forms of social cooperation and solidarity. Nonetheless, the crux of this issue is that 'society as a whole' is not a straightforwardly uncontested concept to which we can easily help ourselves, and thus any choice about scope or scale of measurement will rest on significant contextual assumptions that require critical scrutiny. Thus, it should not be assumed that a smaller scope is a simple solution to this problem, or the other problems we identify in the book.

1.5 CONCLUSION

In this chapter, we have tried to sketch out the conceptual terrain in which 'social cohesion' is discussed and used. Our purpose in doing so, however, has not been to stake out our own position within the various distinctions and approaches we have identified. Rather, it has been to survey the terrain on which we need to organize our attack on the concept as a whole. Our criticism will develop and take shape in the coming chapters. However, before proceeding, we can already observe how several of the features we have discussed contribute to shielding the concept from criticism. Representing it as simply the latest form of a (or even *the*) perennial problem of sociology adds a layer of historical legitimacy and evades the question of why *this* concept emerged at *this* time. The minimal sense that both members of society and state institutions have an interest in society 'holding together' becomes conflated with more substantive values, and the very fact that social cohesion can be used in so many different senses—from thin, particularist and formal to thick, universalist and substantive—contributes to the flexibility and elasticity that makes it popular. As we have already suggested, this is most attractive to politicians who might use it for their own ends, but it also contributes to a sense that, even if we might disagree about the details, 'social cohesion' must refer to *something* and that thing is worth investigating. Meanwhile, whatever that something is slips through one's fingers. In the next chapter we will push further into the social research literature by looking more closely at three influential approaches, two of which can be characterized as universalist and one as particularist.

Chapter 2

From Radars to Regimes

Concepts of Social Cohesion in Focus

In this chapter, we build on the analysis of the previous chapter by looking at some prominent theoretical approaches that respond to the context of the rise of interest in social cohesion in policy. Continuing with the theoretical scaffolding developed in chapter 1, the first part of the chapter examines two approaches best described as universalist. These respond to some of the confusions raised by 'social cohesion' in policy discourses by attempting to disentangle and develop a clear and measurable concept. Crucially, they do so in order to present a concept back to policymakers which can then be put to better use. However, in doing so, we argue, they give rise to several points of tension that tend to reproduce, rather than resolve, problems in the policy literature. In attempting to develop an apparently objective, quantifiable, and comparable measure they risk disguising various contestable assumptions about good social cooperation behind a veneer of scientific authority. At the same time, they reproduce both the assumption that social cohesion is a worthwhile policy goal and the confusion about the different levels at which it is understood to be valuable.

In the second, shorter, part of the chapter we examine an example of a particularist approach. Such approaches resist the trend towards universalism by stressing that social cohesion might be compatible with a variety of different components, attitudes, institutions, and practices, depending on their cultural and historical context. While this allows more attention to local details, it also calls into question the value of 'social cohesion' as a concept that can be systematically applied in the policy context, and, we suggest, should lead us to question its value as a distinct concept.

Before proceeding, two caveats are in order: First, by focusing on examples we obviously do not do justice to the enormous breadth of social research on social cohesion. Our exemplars are chosen to capture and elucidate some of the most significant trends and (especially the two universalist ones) because they are among the most common reference points at the intersection between policy and research with which we are most concerned. Second, the distinction between universalist and particularist is a schematic one and, as we will see, in practice universalist and particularist tendencies combine in ways that might challenge this distinction. Nonetheless, this schema, like the exemplars, helps draw out what we consider to be the core issues and tensions in the concept.

2.1 TWO UNIVERSALIST EXAMPLES

Our first example of a broadly universalist approach is that offered by Chan et al. in their 2006 article 'Reconsidering Social Cohesion: Developing a Definition and Analytical Framework for Empirical Research.' This article is widely cited in both policy and social research literature and is framed as a response to some of the earlier confusions in the use of the term, including by the European Union and the Council of Europe. They insist that social cohesion is "meaningful yet inadequately analyzed in the literature."[1] The rise in usage of the term reflects how "politicians and policymakers worldwide have gradually come to recognise [that] new forms of social cleavages necessitate a new form of governance."[2] While this recognition has not yet been accompanied by the necessary clarity that would enable this form of governance, there is no reason to think this impossible. Indeed, "With a more rigorous and clearer definition, 'social cohesion' will become a more meaningful and useful concept in academic policy research."[3]

Thus, for Chan et al.,

> Social cohesion is a state of affairs concerning both the vertical and the horizontal interactions among members of society as characterised by a set of attitudes and norms that includes trust, a sense of belonging and the willingness to participate and help, as well as their behavioural manifestations.[4]

This is designed to reflect several requirements. First, it is supposed to be minimal in scope, offering only "essential components" and not including contingent factors, conditions, or values.[5] Second, it reflects everyday language regarding social cohesion. They argue that this demands seeing social cohesion as a state of affairs rather than a process, and requires a connection between social cohesion and 'sticking together.' The connection between 'sticking together' and trust and willingness to help is represented as a "quasi-tautology, since it is virtually impossible to conceive of a situation in which we say people are 'sticking' together even though they refuse to trust, help or co-operate with each other."[6]

Moreover, they insist that social cohesion must be "spatially specific" and based on "repeated interactions" within a given society, which in turn should be based on the "sovereign state as its unit of analysis."[7] The emphasis on belonging or common identity is thus intended to distinguish social cohesion from spontaneous short-term cooperation among strangers, for example in states of emergency. Social cohesion is understood as a combination of objective and subjective aspects, insofar as it only makes sense if attitudes are manifested in behavior (since "a high level of willingness to cooperate and help would be rather meaningless unless it is also witnessed by substantial [sic] amount of social and political participation"[8]). When it comes to measuring social cohesion, they suggest it should be detected in both subjective beliefs about, and objective behaviors towards, both other groups in society (horizontal) and towards political and social institutions (vertical).[9]

Our second example is the more recent Social Cohesion Radar.[10] This is developed by a group of researchers working for the German *Bertelsmann Stiftung* (who had the foresight to acquire www.social-cohesion.net),[11] and its authors have also produced surveys of social cohesion in the European Foundation for the Improvement of Living and Working Conditions (Eurofound).[12] Significantly, its understanding of social cohesion has been picked up largely unchanged by the German International Development Agency (which we will see in chapter 4). The Radar goes much further than Chan et al. in not only suggesting a measurable concept of social cohesion but by attempting to track it across thirty-four countries (EU member states and several other "Western" members of the OECD—Australia, Israel, Canada, New Zealand, Norway, Switzerland and the United States) over the period 1989–2012. Although developed for the study of these "Western" societies, the same concept was later tracked in Asian societies.[13] Like Chan et al., it deliberately and self-consciously responds to both the rise in policy concerns about social cohesion and the sense that the concept is poorly and inadequately defined. Responding to Bernard's suggestion that social cohesion is a quasi-concept,[14] its authors respond,

> Some 16 years after Bernard's criticism, social cohesion has attained the status of an official policy goal in Germany and elsewhere. The need to define and measure it in a constructive way derives partly from this fact. Bernard's criticism should be taken as an incentive to define and measure cohesion transparently.[15]

The Social Cohesion Radar understands social cohesion as follows:

> Social cohesion is the quality of social cooperation and togetherness of a collective, defined in geopolitical terms, that is expressed in the attitudes and behaviors of its members. A cohesive society is characterized by resilient social

relations, a positive emotional connectedness between its members and the community, and a pronounced focus on the common good.[16]

This divides social cohesion into three domains, which are further divided into three dimensions. Thus, the domain of "social relations" is composed of the dimensions of "social networks," "trust in people," and "acceptance of diversity"; the domain of connectedness contains the dimensions of "identification," "trust in institutions," and "perception of fairness"; and the domain of "focus on the common good" involves "solidarity and helpfulness," "respect for social rules," and "civic participation."[17] These dimensions are measured by means of an extensive use of secondary survey data that tracks both objective and subjective factors. The dimensions, and implicitly social cohesion itself, are thus represented as latent features that cannot be directly measured, but which can be measured indirectly through a "pattern of observed attitudes."[18] They can then be aggregated to track social cohesion as a whole and draw comparisons over time and between countries.

Thus, both universalist accounts stress the need for a measurable and clearly defined concept of social cohesion that can guide policymaking and research. Social cohesion has first to be *isolated* from the various goals and agendas to which it is linked; and only then can it be brought back into policy analysis as something distinct. They thus reflect the need in policy for apparently objective benchmarks and measures with which to assess policies, which in turn leads them towards the language of ontological realism: social cohesion is a 'state of affairs' out there in the world, or something that can be detected through a sophisticated tool which can "see things that are invisible to the naked eye."[19] Moreover, both appear to accept methodological nationalism by assuming that existing nation states are the appropriate 'societies' in which to measure social cohesion.[20] Indeed, the Social Cohesion Radar includes national identification as one of its domains of social cohesion, and tracks this as a single variable even in countries—like Cyprus and Israel, for example—where ideas of 'national belonging' are (to say the least) extremely contested, and where parts of the population living on a given territory are excluded from citizenship.

However, while both accounts can be described as universalist in the sense that they seek to provide unitary definitions of social cohesion and build into it various necessary components, dimensions or indicators, there is an important difference in how they are developed. Chan et al.'s account of social cohesion is intended to be applicable across different societies and aspires to be transhistorical. They explicitly reject the idea that social cohesion requires values such as 'tolerance' or 'respect for diversity' because that might rule out societies held together by other values: a society is clearly imaginable in which "social cohesion would not be promoted by toleration or respect for pluralism; indeed cohesion would be more likely with further homogenization, which could imply intolerance and the purging of dissidents."[21] They challenge the inclusion of 'equality of opportunity' on similar grounds: "It is not difficult to quote from human history numerous examples of highly cohesive and stable societies in which 'equal opportunity' would be an utterly alien notion, not only in theory but also in practice."[22] Their understanding of social cohesion is intended to be 'minimal in scope' (or 'thin' in the sense we used in chapter 1) and to closely match what they consider to be the ordinary language usage of social cohesion (following dictionary definitions).

In contrast, the Social Cohesion Radar is designed explicitly to reflect contemporary debates and concerns. First, the concept is designed to be a composite of the most prominent aspects over which there is broad agreement in existing literature. Against those who would argue that the social cohesion debate is incoherent, the authors argue that it is possible to identify broad agreement on the three aspects that form their core 'domains' of social cohesion. In this sense, the concept appears as a *distillation* of a particular social scientific debate—the reason these dimensions matter is that they are more or less the dimensions that other commentators have settled on.[23] Second, and more significantly for our purposes, the authors stress that "one should refrain from claims of ultimate truth in the definitions of the concept, but rather accept that the definition will always be partly a normative decision which can be changed, depending on the *Zeitgeist*."[24] Thus the concept of social cohesion is an abstraction, or idealization, that both *distils* popular ideas about what social cohesion *is*, and reflects ideas about what it *should be*.

This introduces a significant tension, which we will develop further below. While the Social Cohesion Radar understands itself as offering a partially normative definition that reflects a *Zeitgeist*, it nonetheless represents it as something that can be measured using a sophisticated tool: "Unlike directly observable characteristics such as, for example, body temperature, cohesion is not an objective condition that can be easily measured. Accordingly, the measurement instrument developed for this study is complex."[25] There are two parallel risks here, especially when the concept becomes removed from a purely scientific concept and handed back to policymakers to put into use: First, that the particular normative *Zeitgeist* reflected by the concept might not be as uncontroversial as this implies—that the values it rests on are presented as broadly agreed and beyond contestation when they may in fact be contestable and contested. Second, that this normative status disappears from view entirely, and the concept becomes treated *as if it were* the kind of transhistorical and transcultural concept that Chan et al. propose. This is of course particularly problematic given that the Social Cohesion Radar was developed for the study of Western countries, but its set of domains and dimensions are also being applied in international development contexts and to the study of Asian countries.

2.1.1 Diversity and Shared Values

Above, we contrasted our two examples of universalist accounts based on whether they approach social cohesion as a transhistorical concept or as an intellectual construct dependent on the cultural *Zeitgeist*. It would be tempting, then, to understand this as a dispute about the normative status of social cohesion, with the Social Cohesion Radar acknowledging that it is a necessarily normative concept and Chan et al. seeing it as purely descriptive. This, however, would be too hasty, eliding the various complex and conflicting ways in which normativity enters these accounts.

As we have seen, Chan et al. exclude values such as tolerance and equality of opportunity from their definition. Thus, social cohesion does not depend on any specific values, and may even be compatible with *either* a homogeneity *or* a diversity of values, so long as these encourage (or at least do not inhibit) trust and cooperation. When it comes to the latter point, the authors of the Social Cohesion Radar agree: "We exclude shared values from our concept of cohesion firstly because it is unclear which values people would have to share to guarantee cohesion and because we are not convinced that cohesion in modern societies requires homogeneity of values at all."[26] They suggest, invoking Durkheim, that models of social cohesion that depend on strong value homogeneity are outdated and "fail to account for the reality of diverse and complex societies."[27] In places, they also seem to agree with Chan et al. about the exclusion of values in general, asserting that "excluding values from the concept allows us to investigate which values affect (and are affected by) social cohesion."[28]

Despite this, however, the Social Cohesion Radar does appear to include one significant value concept in the form of "acceptance of diversity."[29] This is a dimension of social cohesion (in the domain of 'social relations'), and thus it contributes directly to social cohesion's measurement. The more accepting people are of diversity (measured by both their normative attitudes: "Is homosexuality acceptable? Is cultural life enriched by immigrants?"; and beliefs about their society: "Is your city a good place for gays, lesbians and racial/ethnic minorities?"), the more socially cohesive a society is. This raises significant questions. First, the reason for its inclusion seems to oscillate between normative and empirical: The authors explicitly describe its inclusion as a "value judgement,"[30] but they also imply that it is connected to an empirical claim (following Durkheim) that "Modern societies are based not on 'mechanical solidarity' rooted in similarity, but on 'organic solidarity' rooted in diversity and mutual interdependence."[31]

Second, while they present the decision to include acceptance of diversity as a value judgment, the authors suggest that this is compatible with excluding shared values from social cohesion itself. Thus, sharing acceptance of diversity does not constitute sharing values (contra Chan et al. who explicitly see "tolerance or respect for diversity" as a value that need not be shared).[32] This, on its face, is puzzling, and might be interpreted in various ways. The first is suggested when the authors of the Social Cohesion Radar begin to investigate the relationships *between* social cohesion and "individual-level value preferences," drawn from the European Social Survey. These values are understood as "the guiding principles people follow in their lives" and are grouped under headings such as "Universalism," "Benevolence," "Tradition," "Hedonism," "Conformity," and "Security."[33] This, however, seems to introduce a genuine risk of circularity, since the value of "universalism" is described as "Understanding, appreciation, tolerance, and protection for the welfare of all people and nature."[34] Can this value really have been said to have been analytically separated from a definition of social cohesion that includes acceptance of diversity? It is perhaps unsurprising that this value is seen to be correlated with social cohesion (although so are "benevolence," "hedonism," "stimulation," and "self-direction").[35]

An alternative way to understand this, however, would be to see the Social Cohesion Radar's rejection of shared values as a rejection of something like first-order values, or perhaps something close to 'conceptions of the good life' or Rawlsian 'comprehensive doctrines.'[36] Thus social cohesion would not require shared Catholic or Islamic values, or shared understandings of family, duty, and social role. In this context, acceptance of diversity would be a second-order value in the sense that it enables a minimum normative consensus while allowing people to pursue different first-order values and conceptions of the good life. While this is not a distinction they make directly (indeed, it is one that the examples in the previous paragraph appear to conflate), it is broadly compatible with their commitment to Durkheimian organic solidarity.

A particular example of how these assumptions shape outcomes can be found in the treatment of national identification. This is included as a dimension of social cohesion, but the analysis of the Radar reveals it to be something of an outlier. Some countries score far higher in the connectedness domain than they do for overall cohesion, primarily because they have particularly high national identification. Thus, the authors suggest, "Identification behaves as an atypical dimension of social cohesion: High scores on it guarantee by no means a high rating for social cohesion overall."[37] Identification thus sticks out as an aspect that was theoretically identified with social cohesion, but which does not empirically accompany its other dimensions. Does this mean it is in fact *not* a dimension of social cohesion? The authors speculate that, while identification with one's country "reflects Durkheim's idea of mechanical solidarity . . . the other eight dimensions tap into aspects of Durkheim's organic solidarity, which emphasises individual dignity, equality of opportunity, and social justice."[38] Thus, national identification *really is* the odd one out, because it is rooted in a different kind of solidarity that (following Durkheim) "post-industrial democracies may no longer need in order to sustain social cohesion."[39] However this is not particularly surprising, since the definition of social cohesion was intended at the outset to reflect organic solidarity more than mechanical solidarity. It is thus hard to escape the feeling that this tells us more about the compatibility of national identification and liberal values than it does about something specific called social cohesion. The point here is not that such analysis is completely useless. Indeed, it is a striking finding that national identification does not seem to correlate with a range of other things, perhaps most notably perceptions of trust and fairness (although, again, the fact that two of these outlier countries are Israel and Cyprus should raise serious questions about which nation is being identified with). This is a point that can be mobilized against those who would seek to respond to perceived threats by demanding greater identification with the nation. It is less clear, though, what is achieved by continuing to maintain these factors together under a single category. Indeed, the fact that the authors felt the need to include national identification in the first place shows the concept's ambivalence, which—rather than forming an impetus to further refine and develop 'social cohesion'—might instead give us pause about continuing to invoke it at all.

We can increasingly see, then, how, despite its desire to compare across different societies, the Social Cohesion Radar appears to track a very specific, culturally determined vision of what social cohesion is, rooted not only in a certain idea of modernity, but also certain ideas of liberalism. Social cohesion thus becomes increasingly identified with a particular vision of a good society. Before we pursue this further in the next section, however, it is important to note that treating acceptance of diversity as either an empirical requirement or a second-order (and perhaps therefore less controversial) value can miss the way that it is often tacitly linked to more chauvinistic and exclusionary accounts of 'Western civilization' and of certain national identities, reflecting a particular vision of social group identity. For example, "tolerance for those of other faiths and beliefs" was included on a list of Fundamental British Values promoted by the British government since 2014, which is linked explicitly to counter-terrorism strategies and narratives of the 'end of multiculturalism' that single out Muslim communities as particularly problematic.[40] With such examples in mind, it is not hard to see how, when shifted to the world of policy, the idea that social cohesion requires acceptance of diversity might generate new exclusions and single out particular groups.[41]

2.1.2 The Value of Social Cohesion

In addition to the presence of values in defining and measuring social cohesion, however, there is the normative status of social cohesion itself. Here once again the comparison can be instructive. Chan et al. describe social cohesion as one social value among many, which "may indeed be in conflict with other values or goods, such as diversity, pluralism and creativity."[42] This means that societies might have different preferences about the level of social cohesion they wish to maintain, and that there may be trade-offs between different social goods, implying at least some degree of comparability and commensurability between them. The Social Cohesion Radar also assumes that social cohesion is valuable in its own right, asserting, "Conducting such a study, in itself, suggests that social cohesion is a valuable property of a collectivity of people."[43] However, they appear to go further, in allowing the desirability of social cohesion itself to shape its definition. Thus, the authors assert, "We strive to prevent our definition from permitting any kind of exclusion in society. It is our aim to conceptualize an inclusive form of social cohesion that not only accepts a multitude of lifestyles and identities but views them as a strength."[44] However, it is worth stressing that neither account *has to* treat social cohesion as a value in its own right. It is simply not true that studying social cohesion assumes it is a valuable property, and it is revealing that this comment passes without scrutiny. After all, social cohesion could just as easily have been conceptualized as an entirely neutral feature of society on which diverse social goods rest, perhaps to different degrees. This would still allow for questions of balancing, but without social cohesion being traded off against other values.

This is particularly important because on both accounts social cohesion is not only *a good thing* but is also *good for* many other good things.[45] This is clearest in the Social Cohesion Radar, which compares changes in their index of social cohesion over time with various other social phenomena to suggest relationships between social cohesion and its causes and consequences. Thus, they can point to "a causal loop" between wealth and social cohesion: "Wealthier societies are indeed more cohesive, but at the same time, more cohesive societies appear to be more productive."[46] They argue that immigration does not clearly correlate with social cohesion: "Immigration thus is not a threat to social cohesion. Neither do more cohesive societies deter or attract migrants."[47] Inequality undermines social cohesion, but social cohesion does not lead to greater equality. Social cohesion also seems to lead to improvements on the human development index, leading them to conclude (somewhat exaggeratedly) that social cohesion "is thus instrumental for human progress."[48] Social cohesion is also strongly linked to the somewhat nebulous 'knowledge economy': "It thus appears that progress in education, innovation, and communication technologies strengthens cohesion, but also that more cohesive societies manage to make greater advances towards a knowledge economy."[49] Most importantly, social cohesion is linked to subjective individual well-being: "strong social cohesion is a valuable property, since it is conducive to people's happiness and life satisfaction"—this is later elided into simply claiming "Cohesion is happiness"[50]—and "a cohesive society is a crucial societal condition for a positive life evaluation."[51] Finally, social cohesion is also negatively correlated with religiosity but positively correlated with post-materialist values—yet another understanding of value, though discussed under the rubric of culture.[52]

We will not dispute these relationships; nor do we wish to argue that they offer no meaningful insights. But it is striking that they suggest an additional set of answers to the question "Why care about social cohesion?" Social cohesion is *already* assumed to be minimally valuable and worthy of investigation; in the Social Cohesion Radar it already has some important second-order values built into it; it is now also represented as instrumental for several other valuable things. We should care about it because we should care about our society holding together; we should care about it because social cohesion means something good; and we should care about it because it helps us get other good things. The point here is not that this is incoherent: it is possible for something to be both good and instrumental for other good things (sport and health have this relationship, for example). Likewise, it can help to be able to isolate which element of the relationship you want to focus on, which might in turn shift over time (Do I play tennis for my health or am I concentrating on my health so as to play better tennis?). However, what this shows is that the normativity of social cohesion is *over-determined*. This *normative overdetermination* allows social cohesion, and concepts like it, to become rather slippery. It creates room for ambiguity about why social cohesion is being pursued There is no *a priori* reason why these distinctions cannot be kept in view and this slippage avoided. But as we move to considering social cohesion as a concept in politics and policy, and these concepts become attached to real institutions with interests and agendas, this slipperiness is increasingly open to misunderstanding and manipulation.

Alongside this normative overdetermination, the regular tendency to instrumentally link social cohesion to other goods seems to reduce the significance of sociality and social relations to mere means or vehicles for development. This kind of shift to instrumentality is visible in the Eurofound's report on *Social Cohesion and Well-Being in Europe* written by three of the authors of the Social Cohesion Radar. It emphasizes the value of social cohesion *for* well-being: "If subjective well-being is the ultimate good that the institutional arrangement of societies should aim to provide, then social cohesion emerges as a necessary condition."[53] Subjective well-being in turn appears not only as a good in itself but as "an important benchmark for evaluating human progress."[54] Here we can see a different kind of potential slippage, as the good for which social cohesion is valuable itself becomes instrumentally valuable in a kind of chain of instrumentality, with the value of social relations themselves increasingly diminished.

2.1.3 Participation, Civil Society and Depoliticization

So far, we have emphasized the differences between these two universalist accounts. Strikingly, though, when it comes to the indicators used to measure social cohesion, there is a high level of overlap. Despite Chan et al.'s claim that they see social cohesion as entirely independent of liberal values of tolerance, when they come to identify indicators for horizontal-subjective cohesion, they include the question "Would you be willing to cooperate with your colleagues if he/she has the following background: lower/higher social stratum, gay/straight, different political view, new immigrant, lives on welfare?" This question is narrower than those posed by the Social Cohesion Radar (which concern not merely willingness to cooperate but willingness to live alongside), but it already suggests a closer overlap in practice, and raises the question of how genuinely transhistorical this indicator is—since it would seem to rule out societies united, for example, by homophobia or hostility to migrants.[55]

A further significant overlap appears concerning those objective measures of social cohesion that relate to society as a whole—in other words, the behaviors that are understood to be expressions and manifestations of subjective willingness to work together and cooperate. Here, despite the different taxonomies, they settle on a very similar list of indicators. In the case of the Social Cohesion Radar, other than respect for traffic laws, sense of safety and the size of the shadow economy, the domain of 'focus on the common good' is measured through civic participation (wearing a campaign sticker, signing a petition, contacting politicians, voting) and various forms of volunteering and charitable donation. Likewise, for Chan et al. vertical-objective (that is, objective behaviors related to public institutions) cohesion is expressed through voting and participation in strikes and demonstrations (these are notably absent from the Social Cohesion Radar, although even Chan et al. are unclear whether the latter is a positive or negative indicator) whereas horizontal-objective cohesion (objective behaviors between social groups) is measured by "the vibrancy of civil society," again indicated by participating in "community groups, political parties, pressure groups, trade unions, professional societies, churches, clubs, etc." and by volunteering and financial donations.[56]

Crucially, while both examples emphasize the importance of civic and political participation, they seem to be entirely neutral about the nature and character of this participation. Voting for a far-right party counts the same as voting for a liberal one (although it might be cancelled out by expressed hostility to immigrants); a trade union, a community football team, an employer's association and a freemasons' lodge all seem to count towards social cohesion; a petition to gun down migrant boats counts as much as one to renovate a local school. There is a curious weightlessness to this sense of civic participation, reflecting an understanding of participation as essential to a good society but an indifference to its actual content.[57] There is no attention to the particular ideologies that might motivate these forms of participation; or the experiences of exploitation, oppression, or grievance that might give rise to them; or the needs, desires, and interests that might be articulated and expressed through them. Any idea of the 'the common good' here is a distinctly depoliticized one, based largely on helping out, donating to charity, and turning up to vote.

To take a concrete example, a recent paper on social cohesion in France identifies the *Gilets Jaunes* movement as both a potential symptom of low social cohesion and a potential underminer of future social cohesion.[58] Defenders of the movement, however, might argue that it is better understood as containing opportunities for developing new forms of democratic participation, engagement, and renewal that go well beyond the limits of existing politics.[59] It is hard to see how a narrow focus on civic participation can even begin to address this question. Either the *Gilets Jaunes* are excluded from measurement entirely or they appear as part of a healthy, engaged citizenry, flattening their complex set of grievances and resentments. While Chan et al. might be right that a willingness to help each other out and cooperate might be understood as tautologically linked to the idea of social cohesion, the link to such a thin notion of participation is far less clear: why should we understand all civic participation as *equally* indicative of social cohesion?[60]

In this context, it is worth saying a little about civil society itself. Civil society is a concept with a long and complex history, but it is often understood as emerging at a specific historical conjuncture connected to the rise of capitalism, liberal politics, and clear conceptual separations between society, the economy, and the state. It thus has deep roots in the political philosophy of modernity, understood variously as describing that which lies outside of the state or as an intermediary space between economy and the state. The term underwent a significant revival in the 1990s in the context of the revolt against state socialism and Latin American dictatorships; it was first conceived as first an oppositional concept, creating breathing space at a distance from the state and resisting the classic division between reform and revolution, and then later as a concept for state construction, seen especially in terms of providing reflexive constraints on state power.[61] Despite all these complexities, the accounts we focus on here tend to first subsume a large range of activities under the term civil society (including formal political activities) and assume that the existence of a dynamic civil society is uncomplicatedly positive for social cohesion.

Invoking civil society thus raises a number of problems: First, it offers a particular challenge to Chan et al.'s insistence on a transhistorical account: is civil society similarly to be understood in a transhistorical manner? Was there civil society in the feudal world? In the totalitarian societies they imagine? Did civil society provide for cohesion in state socialist regimes?[62] Conversely, assuming that civil society is always and in all places an indicator of social cohesion suggests that social cohesion is in fact deeply linked to conceptions of liberal modernity. Second, as with the case of acceptance of diversity, civil society is a concept that can sometimes come with its own exclusions, particularly of non-citizens and those understood as 'uncivil.' Third, conceiving of civil society in terms of undifferentiated activity fails to distinguish between forms of civil society activity that are in conflict with existing social order and those that reinforce and support it. This especially ignores a tradition of thinking in which civil society (or at least some elements of it) provides a challenge to existing society, by embodying alternative structures and social relations to it (we will return to this in our final chapter).[63] In this way, it risks giving civil society an essentially instrumental role in maintaining social order (and whatever else social cohesion is instrumentally valuable for). The conception of civil society as something that either reflexively limits the state or helps transcend it now appears instead as something that contributes to the state's stability without meaningfully transforming it.[64]

Of course, it is possible for defenders of these approaches to respond that these are merely some indicators among many. They would not, of course, be so naive as to suggest that a society which was full of civic participation but at the same time demonstrated high levels of mistrust and corruption was socially cohesive. Civic participation would simply be balanced out by the other indicators, leading to low cohesion overall. Our point, however, is that they reveal some of the dubious assumptions that underlie much of this discourse, which we should be particularly wary of when they are put into practice by actually existing states and institutions.

2.1.4 Drawing Together the Criticisms

We are now in a position to draw together some of these critical points of tension in these universalist accounts. Chan et al. offer an account of social cohesion as a transhistorical feature of societies, a state of affairs in which society holds together that can in principle be identified in any historical (or even imaginable) society. They thus offer a relatively thin conception that seeks to exclude various values and represents social cohesion as compatible with different ideological tendencies. However, when it comes to measuring social cohesion they present criteria that are strikingly historically specific, most notably regarding attitudes of tolerance and conceptions of civil society. Thus, they risk smuggling in quite specific understandings of the social under the guise of historical generality. In contrast, the Social Cohesion Radar is explicit in developing a normatively shaped and historically specific understanding of social cohesion that is appropriate for diverse modern societies. However, at the same time, they build around these normative assumptions a complex apparatus of measurement and comparison that treats it *as if* it were a quasi-objective property that can be quantified, compared, and made commensurate across different national contexts and assigned causal efficacy. Thus, while they proceed in different directions, both accounts risk presenting an ideological contestable view of good social cooperation as either purely descriptive or as sufficiently uncontroversial to be accepted and applied neutrally in policy.

At the same time, these accounts continue to reflect the idea that social cohesion is a valuable policy goal, but they do so in ways that tend to confuse the different levels at which it is valuable. This is most clear in the Social Cohesion Radar, where social cohesion appears as normatively defined and both intrinsically and instrumentally valuable. This normative overdetermination risks two distinct problems: First, when it is reintroduced to the policy context it presents policymakers with a variety of different reasons for promoting social cohesion and creates opportunities for both unconscious slippages and conscious manipulations that allow it to be linked to various agendas in ways that obscure rather than illuminate. Second, it tends to inflate the value of social cohesion itself, allowing it to increasingly approximate the idea of a good society and thus making policies undertaken in its name harder to contest. Indeed, at one point the authors of the Social Cohesion Radar boldly state, "Simply put, the greater the cohesion, the better."[65]

Last, but not least, when social cohesion is framed as of instrumental value, it tends to reduce the significance of social interactions to a mere means for other goods. This tendency combines with the demands of measurement and quantification to produce strikingly thin, depoliticized notions of social activity and participation, which (deliberately) abstract from the specific ideological, historical, and social content of that activity. Ideas such as 'civil society' or 'the common good' become reduced to abstract ideas of 'participation,' measured quantitatively without regard to people's goals and understandings.[66] At worst, we might worry that this amounts to a strangely depoliticized view of social cohesion. This is perhaps summed up by the authors of the Social Cohesion Radar's remark, already quoted in chapter 1, that in the famous French revolutionary motto of *"liberté, égalité, fraternité,"* the "latter goal . . . seems to be the call of the French Revolution for a cohesive society."[67] There we argued that this depends on a strangely denuded understanding of fraternity. Here we can go further: it assumes that a revolutionary slogan can be transformed into a concept of governance. The desire for an apparently objective and neutral policy concept strips it of its rich historical meanings and interpretations, and reduces its significance to the instrumental purposes of states and governments.

2.2 THE PARTICULARIST ALTERNATIVE

In the previous section, we focused our criticism on universalist approaches. In what remains of the chapter, we look at an example of an alternative, *particularist*, approach. If universalist accounts of social cohesion respond to the general confusion about its meaning by attempting to clarify and define it in general terms, then particularist approaches respond by suggesting that social cohesion ought to be understood as manifested differently in different social and cultural contexts. A prominent example of this is Andy Green and Jan Germen Janmaat's *Regimes of Social Cohesion: Societies and the Crisis of Globalisation.* They propose a definition of social cohesion designed to avoid several of the problems already discussed. Some of these are the same as those to which the universalist approaches are responding, that is, confusion of causes, components and effects, and confusion about the scope of application. Others, though, are features of universalist approaches we identified above, most notably the role of normativity and the tendency to aggregate various positive features that might otherwise be unrelated. Green and Janmaat criticize the use of social cohesion "as a signifier for a positive condition for which we ought to strive."[68] Beyond general methodological concerns about the relationship between normative concepts and objectivity, they stress in particular how this approach leads either to ignoring salient aspects of cohesion that are ruled out by the normative definition, or to the assumption that cohesion is an uncomplicated good.

In order to avoid these pitfalls of universalist accounts, Green and Janmaat characterize social cohesion as follows:

> Social cohesion refers to the property by which whole societies, and the individuals within them, are bound together through the action of specific attitudes, behaviours, rules and institutions which rely on consensus rather than pure coercion.[69]

The definition avoids identifying any of the "specific attitudes" or "behaviors" at stake, leaving out even the relatively thin notions such as "trust, a sense of belonging and the willingness to participate and help" identified by Chan et al.[70] However, social cohesion remains distinguished from mere coercion and thus societies (if they exist) held together solely by coercion are not cohesive.[71]

Green and Janmaat's approach to social cohesion is designed to help them distinguish between different *regimes* of social cohesion. Regimes are defined as "relatively durable (but not immutable) configurations of social attitudes and behaviors contributing to society-wide social bonding that are underpinned by particular institutional arrangements."[72] They are ideal types, and thus should not be expected to map perfectly onto specific actually existing states. Since social cohesion is a state-level phenomenon, they are understood in terms of national systems, but "any national regime will also be dependent on supra-national global and regional structures, systems and flows, which must be accounted for"[73]—although *how* they are accounted for is somewhat unclear.

They identify three such regimes: (1) *liberal*, characterized by Britain and the United States; (2) *social market*, characterized by France and Germany; and (3) *social democratic*, as in the Nordic countries (though they also reflect on the possibility of a fourth 'East Asian' regime). Loosely, these can be summarized as follows.

Liberal regimes have a strong emphasis on individual property rights and see social cohesion as emergent from civil society and the free market. Market interference is kept to the minimum required to stabilize the market and offset its worst consequences. Labor markets are flexible and wages are set largely by supply and demand, rather than by sector-wide bargaining agreements. Welfare policies tend to be less universalistic and more means-tested. High levels of inequality are tolerated and justified by a strong sense of meritocracy, and by rising wages and prosperity, based on high employment and economic growth.

Social market regimes, drawing on a republican political tradition, see the state as having a greater role in securing the conditions for social cohesion. This regime "tends to institutionalise the sources of social cohesion,"[74] by which is intended a recognition of them as explicit concerns of state institutions. Companies are seen as having responsibilities to their employees and society through a broader conception of 'stakeholders' (rather than merely 'shareholders'). This also suggests that there are widespread collective bargaining agreements that promote solidarity among various groups and lead to more equal wages. Welfare policies are often rooted in a complex network of employment-based insurance, where solidaristic effects are often combined with hierarchical and patriarchal assumptions and relatively little redistribution, combining solidarity among the employed and the relative exclusion of the unemployed.

Social democratic regimes are characterized by an ideological commitment to equality and an active pursuit of it as a value in its own right. They share many of the solidaristic elements of the social market but can be distinguished by a much higher level of income equality and much more active state intervention in encouraging employment and redistributing wealth. This is underpinned by a deep commitment to comprehensive education, with extremely egalitarian outcomes. Such societies are also marked by a high level of trust, something which they suggest they should "probably include alongside relative equality among the characteristic features of the social democratic regime of social cohesion."[75]

This indicates clearly the difference between Green and Janmaat's approach and that of the Social Cohesion Radar. While both distinguish different regimes of social cohesion in the sense of broad regional groupings, the Social Cohesion Radar does so on the basis of the same set of indicators, allowing them to compare levels of social cohesion between these regimes, and rank them as more or less cohesive. In contrast, Green and Janmaat's approach precludes such comparison because different indicators have different valences in different regimes. The examples of 'trust' and 'equality' are usefully illustrative of their approach. In their quantitative analysis, trust (measured by subjective reporting) and equality (based on objective measures) are identified as *components* of social democratic regimes, whereas social market regimes have a negative relationship with trust and no relationship to equality, and liberal regimes have a negative relationship to equality and no relationship to trust.[76] This method of analysis extends to various other "components of social cohesion regimes" including preference for freedom over equality (or vice versa), crime (considered, somewhat bafflingly, an "essential part" of the liberal regime), gender equality (measured by subjective attitudes and seen as a component of liberal and social democratic regimes and absent from social market regimes) and ethnic tolerance (considered a component of the liberal regime but incidental to the other two).[77]

While these regimes are initially *presented* through qualitative analysis of their ideological traditions and institutions and only later through quantitative analysis, Green and Janmaat emphasize that their analysis is iterative. They do not assume such regimes and then go looking for evidence of their existence. Rather "the quantitative analysis has in fact been constitutive in the development of the theoretical models."[78] Nonetheless, their choice of where to look is clearly influenced by prior categorizations of European regimes, most obviously that of the literature on welfare regimes and varieties of capitalism, which emphasizes distinctive patterns of welfare provision and approaches towards ownership.[79] Thus, when it comes to the relevant institutional features, they focus narrowly on "the laws and regulations governing property and ownership, including company law"; "the organization of the labour market"; and "the arrangements for wage-setting and income redistribution and the welfare system."[80]

They are clear that this choice is somewhat arbitrary, noting that "areas such as immigration and race relations policy, housing policy, and education would also be relevant but for reasons of space and time we do not seek to cover all these here, important though they may be to the underlying foundations of social cohesion."[81] Yet again, however, this methodological choice risks serious blindspots: if we are to speak meaningfully of whole regimes of cohesion, then simply to bracket out elements relevant to foundations risks completely mischaracterizing such regimes. Why assume that societies that share a labour market structure also share education or housing policy? And if not, why does the former indicate a shared regime and the latter not? In fact, Green and Janmaat *do* reintroduce education policy when discussing its distinctive role in social democratic regimes[82] and do discuss issues of immigration and cultural diversity when discussing threats to the social market regime.[83] It is thus hard to escape the suspicion that they might have divided up these regimes quite differently had they focused on other aspects.[84] This should push us to question the value of hard and fast distinctions of regime, since the idea of a distinct 'regime-type' is clearly heavily contingent on particular frames of analysis and points of reference.[85]

Strikingly, Green and Janmaat conclude by discussing a number of challenges to these regimes. This is placed in the broader context that tends to motivate discussions of social cohesion, namely a perception of its decline caused by "globalization, individuation, individualism, inequality, demographic change and generational splits."[86] They admit that if it is possible to talk of regimes converging around general, global trends and about general threats to social cohesion, then this puts pressure on the notion of regimes itself. They conclude, however, that "the evidence we have on trends in different aspects of social cohesion suggest a mixture of both convergence and divergence."[87] They conclude this on the basis of analysing trends in "measures of social trust, political trust, tolerance and perceptions of conflict between groups."[88]

While mentioning several regime-specific threats—such as declining belief in meritocracy under liberal regimes, ethnic and cultural diversity under social market regimes, and long-term pressures on the welfare state under social democratic regimes—their discussion of trust reveals an apparent inconsistency. They see trust as in general decline across all regions *except* those identified as part of social democracy:

In as much as trust is an important measure for social cohesion, these trends in levels of trust would appear to confirm, at least partially, the general theories discussed above, which posit universal and convergent changes in levels of social cohesion. However, there is a major exception. Levels of trust rose significantly in the Nordic group of countries between 1985 and 2005 and continued to rise after this in Sweden until 2008.[89]

Yet trust was earlier not seen as a necessary feature of liberal regimes at all. It is therefore hard to understand why declining trust suddenly appears as a threat to social cohesion *in those regimes*, and indeed why declining trust has suddenly reappeared as an "important measure of social cohesion" *tout court*. Why this reversion to the language of social cohesion *in general* after taking such care to avoid it? It appears that social cohesion's close intellectual connection to notions of decline and threat continues to shape even those accounts that resist the idea that it can be easily compared across national and cultural contexts, pushing them back towards universalism despite themselves.

Stepping back from the details, we can see how the particularist approach tries to avoid the universalist pitfalls and provide a more descriptive, formalist and context-specific approach to social cohesion. Rather than assuming that a given factor contributes to social cohesion in the same way across all societies, they can be understood as interacting differently across different contexts to form particular combinations that nonetheless contribute to social stability. This thus resists the distillation of social cohesion into a single essence and the normative overdetermination that inflates social cohesion's value, and at the same time makes more visible its connection to ideological values in specific contexts. However, at least in the example we have discussed, when it comes to specifying these contexts in the form of regimes it remains shaped by several contestable assumptions that might have been spelled out quite differently. While, of course, any investigation has to start somewhere and make some methodological assumptions, this should lead us further towards caution about drawing broad conclusions about something called 'social cohesion.' Indeed, the more that particularism pushes us towards context specific investigations about how societies hold together and reproduce themselves, the more we might wonder whether 'social cohesion' simply gets in the way.

2.3 CONCLUSION

In this chapter, we have looked more closely at three specific attempts to conceptualize social cohesion in the context of social research. Two of these—characterized as universalist—respond directly to the rise of social cohesion as a policy concept by attempting to present a measurable and operationalizable concept to policymakers. However, we suggested that such accounts tend to reinforce some of the problems of the policy literature by presenting contestable and historically specific understandings of the social as if they were measurable and objective properties and both inflate the value of social cohesion itself while depoliticizing and flattening complex forms of social participation by reducing them to means for social cohesion. While such accounts present themselves as clarifying and correcting the confusions of policy literature, they often serve only to reinforce these confusions and (even worse) to hide them behind a veneer of scientific legitimacy. In contrast, the particularist approach we examined resists the desire to collapse social cohesion into a single concept that can be easily compared and tracked across different social contexts. However, precisely because of this, it raises the question of whether 'social cohesion' remains a meaningful term at all. First, it becomes hard to generalize in policy terms either through a one 'one size fits all' approach or by ranking and comparing countries (or regions) in terms of their level of cohesiveness. More broadly, the more that particularism pushes towards a focus on specific contexts, the more that the value of 'social cohesion' as a distinctive concept begins to dissolve.

While our focus in this chapter has been mostly on theories of social cohesion in social research, our concern has not primarily been with the explanatory value of those theories *per se*, but with the way in which they interact with, shape, and are shaped by policy concerns. If, as we have stressed in this chapter, social researchers see their role as disentangling the concept of social cohesion from its messy articulations in order to present a usable concept in policy, such concepts cannot be judged only by their theoretical consistency but also by how they become used. In the following two chapters, we will shift our focus towards the policy side of this dynamic, to look at how the concept has been taken up and shaped by policy institutions at the European and international level.

Chapter 3

Between Economic Growth and Social Rights

European Policy Discourse

In the previous chapter, we saw how social researchers responded to the rise of 'social cohesion' in policy discourse by clarifying and instrumentalizing the concept. In this chapter, we will step back to fill in some more of the details about that rise. In particular, we trace the trajectory of the concept across the two main supra-national organizations in Europe, the European Union (EU) and the Council of Europe (CoE) over the past thirty years. We focus on these organizations in part because of their significance in forming and influencing policy at both the national and regional level, but also because they form an important part of the broader story of social cohesion's rise. It is frequently the definitions and approaches of these institutions (alongside those discussed in the following chapter) that are responded to and criticized in the literature, and they thus shape, even if negatively, the way the concept is used and defined.[1] Moreover, as we shall see, the comparison of the two institutions is also instructive for seeing the quite different ways in which 'social cohesion' has been constructed. These organizations both represent a socially cohesive society as necessary, but do so in service of quite different goals, and thus construct different visions and policy agendas around this idea. In keeping with our approach in this book, our goal here is not to suggest that one of these is better than another, but to use the comparisons to point to tensions in the concept. Indeed, as we will argue later, the very fact that such different projects can be subsumed under the label of 'social cohesion' ought to give us pause for thought.

Before discussing the specific organizations, let us set the context. In both organizations, social cohesion is framed as a policy concern from the early 1990s onwards. This is a period marked by the collapse of the Soviet Union and the end of the Cold War that had shaped assumptions about international relations and economic development. In Central and Eastern Europe, the Revolutions of 1989 brought about a change of political regime in the former communist states which launched a long process of their integration into the political, economic, and military structures of the West. In the Balkans, Yugoslavia began to break apart through violent conflicts that caused tens of thousands of casualties and a wave of migration. These were easily framed in terms of failures of social cohesion in the older regimes (Berger-Schmitt remarks that "the former Soviet Union or the former Yugoslavia are good examples of possible consequences of deficiencies in certain aspects of social cohesion."[2]) and *also* as generating potential new threats in the form of refugees and economic migrants.

At the same time, however, there was a growing sense of threat to social cohesion from *within* the states of Western Europe connected to the rapid economic restructuring that had begun in the 1980s. For example, around the turn of the 1990s, the European Foundation for the Improvement of Living and Working Conditions (today known as 'Eurofound') conducted a number of research initiatives under the heading of 'social cohesion,' presented in a booklet called *Bridging the Gulf* with the subtitle *Improving Social Cohesion in Europe: The Work of the European Foundation for the Improvement of Living and Working Conditions, 1984–1993*. This observes that the rapid and profound social, economic, and political change of that time "brought benefits to the great majority of Europe's citizens, in the form of new opportunities, wider choices, greater reward and satisfaction from work, and a better quality of life. . . . [Yet] the positive effects for some have been paralleled by negative effects for others: what are new chances and choices for some are dangers and difficulties for these others."[3] The gulf between the disadvantaged and those who are benefiting from change becomes even wider as the advantaged move forward and the former become the marginalised and excluded—narrowing the gulf becomes a matter of improving social cohesion in Europe.

As we will see, this framing of internal threats to cohesion in terms of a gap between included and excluded, or those who move with the change and those that are left behind by it, repeats frequently across both institutions. At the same time, however, they understand both the nature of these threats and the solutions to them in strikingly divergent ways.

3.1 GROWTH AND EMPLOYMENT—SOCIAL COHESION POLICY OF THE EUROPEAN UNION

The idea of social cohesion has been a part of European Union policy discourse since its creation. The 1992 *Treaty on European Union* (Maastricht Treaty), which brought the EU into being, already commits to "develop and pursue its actions leading to the strengthening of its economic and social cohesion" in order to reduce disparities between the levels of development of the various regions as well as various groups and communities in Europe.[4] The commitment to strengthening social cohesion has remained high on the EU policy agenda until the present day, demonstrated by the 2021 EU Porto Social Summit's concluding declaration, which states, "More than ever, Europe must be the continent of social cohesion and prosperity."[5] Yet, despite the policy priority ascribed to social cohesion by the EU over the last three decades, there is little if any attempt to specify what social cohesion means and entails across EU policy documents. Thus, one of the most recent EU policy documents—which identifies cohesion as "an underlying value or spirit of European integration as well as the European way of life and decision making"[6] and even conceives of it explicitly as "an aim of the EU"[7]—characterizes social cohesion in generic terms as "keeping various social groups together and offering a future for all people, acknowledging diversity" with the aim "to ensure that people in Europe stick together."[8] Social cohesion is represented as the opposite of "the drifting apart of societal groups in the EU, its member states, regions and cities."[9] Looking for a more specific description of what cohesion—as an 'overall value of the EU' entails—the reader of the document is left with vague statements such as "cohesion is about making people's lives better."[10]

This peculiar combination of social cohesion's high priority and vague specification is one of several constants over the three decades of its use. A second, equally significant constant is the tendency to present social cohesion primarily as an economic imperative or a productive factor which contributes to sustainable economic growth and competitiveness.

This is clearly visible as early as the 1994 white paper *Growth, Competitiveness, Employment: The Challenges and Ways Forward into the 21st Century*. In this document, the EU argues that social cohesion in Europe is threatened by the growing number of individuals and groups who occupy a disadvantaged position in the labor market[11] and warns against the rising level of poverty in Europe which "splits society in two"[12] and results in the emergence of a "two-tier"[13] or "dual" society.[14] In line with its basic assumption that efficiency and productivity is the key to both economic and social progress, the EU suggests that the appropriate response to the risk of a 'dual society' lies in "active employment policy which attaches high priority to the search for an activity or training accessible to everyone rather than the registration of and payment to the employed."[15] Active employment policy is the essence of what this document calls 'active solidarity,' as opposed to the 'passive solidarity' of strong social protection and subsidy payments. The document envisions a "new model of European society" based on "less passive and more active solidarity"[16] and claims that "nothing would be more dangerous than for Europe to maintain structures and customs which foster resignation, refusal of commitment and passivity."[17]

The idea that the EU needs to strive for better social cohesiveness through active employment policy is endorsed also by the 1994 white paper *European Social Policy: A Way Forward for the Union*. The document's basic assumption is that the EU's overall policy objective must be to "give the people of Europe the unique blend of economic well-being, social cohesiveness and high overall quality of life which was achieved in the post-war period."[18] This 'unique blend' should be achieved by "continuing productivity gains, which will enable the Union to reconcile high social standards with the capacity to compete in global markets. . . . The key resource will be a well-educated and highly motivated and adaptable working population."[19] The EU views the millions of Europeans living below the poverty line and the endemic social exclusion and marginalization of many social groups as a threat to social cohesion, however, this threat is presented primarily as an obstacle on the way to the greater "efficiency of European society".[20] The document argues that "the Union simply cannot afford to lose the contribution of marginalized groups to society as a whole." Therefore, "the Union needs to ensure that the most vulnerable (people excluded from social and economic life, young people unable to find a foothold in the economy, long-term unemployed, disabled and older people, for example) are not excluded from the benefits of—and from making an active contribution to—the economic strength of a more integrated Europe."[21] Despite the acknowledgment that social cohesion is also "an important goal in its own right," the EU stresses its role as "a key factor contributing to economic success," arguing that "regions which are unable to mobilise the economic potential of large sections of their population are handicapped in the increasingly competitive global market, while disparities can breed social unrest which itself can damage economic performance."[22]

In its 2000 *Lisbon Strategy*, the EU commits "to become the most competitive and dynamic knowledge-based economy in the world capable of sustainable economic growth with more and better jobs and greater social cohesion."[23] The *Strategy* envisions a shift to a digital, knowledge-based economy and formulates the corresponding social cohesion policy in terms of 'social investment': "Investing in people and developing an active and dynamic welfare state will be crucial both to Europe's place in the knowledge economy and for ensuring that the emergence of this new economy does not compound the existing social problems of unemployment, social exclusion and poverty."[24] Building on the principle that "the best safeguard against social exclusion is a job" the document calls for an "active and dynamic welfare state" whose role is to ensure that work pays.[25] The EU's 2005 *Social Agenda* accordingly argues that "Europe needs a greater number of active workers, who are also more productive. This will underpin long-term economic growth, combat unemployment and regional disparities and promote social cohesion."[26]

We see how an economy-oriented approach to social cohesion clearly takes the lead in the EU's policy documents from the early 1990s into the 2000s. The EU's effort to think of the social and economic development of Europe as parallel and mutually reinforcing processes seems to persistently prioritize economic progress as the ultimate goal to which social progress can and should contribute. Thus, threats to social cohesion—such as rising levels of poverty and unemployment which 'split society in two'—are presented as 'unacceptable' because they represent obstacles to greater efficiency in European society which should in turn contribute to greater competitiveness of the EU in the globalized world. In these early framings, then, while reference is occasionally made to social cohesion as a value in itself, its value is more commonly subordinated to and made instrumental for ideas of economic efficiency—references to social cohesion's intrinsic value only serve to blur this picture.

In keeping with the economy-oriented approach, a third common factor across these documents is a focus on policy measures aimed at getting people back to work, which suggests that the EU tends to understand social cohesion in terms of the reinsertion of disadvantaged groups and individuals into the labor market. The motif of activation ('active solidarity,' 'active participation') is the cornerstone of EU social cohesion policy discourse and is closely connected to the idea that the unused potential and skills of disadvantaged groups and individuals are a threat to economic development. At the same time, while cohesion is represented as a solution to social exclusion, exclusion itself is represented as exclusion from the labor market, seen less as a problem for the *excluded* (or even a problem of social justice), and more in terms of a waste of human resources that is a problem for the state as a whole.

A final common factor across these three decades is a constant call for making the notion of social cohesion more operationalizable. The EU stresses that "the objectives of full employment, job quality, labour productivity and social cohesion must be reflected in clear and measurable priorities."[27] Yet, already in its *First Report on Economic and Social Cohesion* the EU admits that the notion of social cohesion (in contrast to the notion of economic cohesion) is "more difficult to define in operational terms."[28] In order to make the notion of social cohesion more operationalizable the EU suggests that it "must be distilled into substantive, and measurable, economic and social targets"[29] and calls for ensuring "that effective monitoring, control and evaluation systems are in place."[30] The EU commits to "monitor annually the situation on the basis of a set of indicators showing overall progress towards the objective of a smart, green and inclusive economy delivering high levels of employment, productivity and social cohesion" and to assess member states' reports on the country-level situation.[31] For this purpose the EU introduced a set of eighteen common statistical indicators—the so called 'Laeken Indicators'—which should allow monitoring in a comparable way of Member States' progress towards the EU social cohesion objectives.[32]

Nonetheless, there are some notable shifts in the way in which social cohesion is framed. The 2003 paper *Building the Knowledge Society: Social and Human Capital Interactions* introduces the notion of 'social capital' into the EU's social cohesion policy discourse. It defines 'social capital' as referring to "networks and participation in public life, together with shared norms, values, culture, habits and practices, trust and understanding that facilitate co-operation within or among groups, to pursue shared objectives."[33] The document understands social cohesion as something broader than social capital, referring to "shared values and commitment to a community." It further argues that "more cohesive societies are effective in realizing collective goals because they are better at protecting and including individuals at risk of exclusion, as well as at ensuring open access to relevant resources and benefits. This understanding of social cohesion encompasses outcomes resulting from various factors, including human and social capital interactions."[34] Notably, the document emphasizes the difference between social capital and social cohesion not only in terms of the scope but also in terms of the possible counter-effects of both phenomena. It argues that "specific configurations of social capital can also work against general social cohesion goals; for example, a high level of bonding social capital in close-knit ethnic communities can prevent their members from engaging in other types of relations outside the group; however, too low levels of linking/bridging social capital—and a correlated too short radius of trust—can prevent integration of the group itself into society at large."[35] However, the overarching idea is that the 'good' forms of social capital contribute to the promotion of social cohesion and quality of life in the "networked society."[36] This positive view of the relationship between social capital and social cohesion goes on to frame the resolution of the Council of the European Union *Social and Human Capital in the Knowledge Society: Learning, Work, Social Cohesion and Gender*. Surprisingly, the resolution does not seem to pay any attention to the above-mentioned differences between the notions of social cohesion and social capital. Instead, it simply stresses "the importance of formal and informal social networks, including digital networks, for social cohesion and the balance between flexibility, security and quality of life" and invites the commission to "pay special attention to the social and human capital aspects in all its on-going policies and initiatives."[37]

Following the financial crisis of 2008, the EU began to link these ideas to the concept of social investment. In his preface to the 2010 document *Europe 2020: A European Strategy for Smart, Sustainable and Inclusive Growth*, the then president of the European Commission, José Manuel Barroso reflects the grave situation in Europe after the crisis in terms of "new pressures on our social cohesion," concluding, "Europe needs to get back on track. Then it must stay on track. That is the purpose of *Europe 2020*. It's about more jobs and better lives. It shows how Europe has the capacity to deliver smart, sustainable and inclusive growth, to find the path to create new jobs and to offer a sense of direction to our societies."[38] The *Strategy*'s key priority of "inclusive growth" is defined as "empowering people through high levels of employment, investing in skills, fighting poverty and modernising labour markets, training and social protection systems so as to help people anticipate and manage change, and build a cohesive society."[39]

This approach was further spelled out in *Towards Social Investment for Growth and Cohesion: Including Implementing the European Social Fund 2014–2020*. Starting from the assumption that "future economic growth and competitiveness require investing in human capital,"[40] the document advocates a growth model which includes "a social investment approach" meaning "investment in social policies that strengthen human capital development."[41] The European Commission contends that the EU member states, faced with structural long-term challenges, "need to adapt to ensure the adequacy and sustainability of their social systems and their contribution to stabilising the economy." In particular, "if a person can temporarily not find work, the focus should be on improving their capabilities with a view of them returning to the labour market.".[42] Despite the allusion to 'cohesion' in the title, the notion of 'social cohesion' appears only once in the document reflecting a trend to replace 'social cohesion' with 'social inclusion,' and 'cohesive society' with 'inclusive society' across a number of EU policy documents of the 2010s—perhaps reflecting clearer acknowledgement of the hegemony of (economic) inclusion over cohesion. Therefore, the European Commission calls for the implementation of "integrated active inclusion strategies"[43] to be accompanied—in analogy to the stronger economic governance and enhanced fiscal surveillance in member states which was introduced by the EU after the global financial crisis—by "improved policy surveillance in the social areas which over time contributes to crisis management, shock absorption and an adequate level of social investment across Europe."[44]

Another new element in the EU's social cohesion policy discourse is the adoption of the notion of 'well-being.' The 2007 Lisbon revision of the *Treaty on European Union* introduces a change to Article 2 of the treaty by inserting the notion of well-being. The revised wording reads as follows: "The Union's aim is to promote peace, its values and the well-being of its peoples."[45] The EU connects the promotion of the well-being of European citizens to the question of social cohesion and progress, based on the assumption that "there are widespread expectations that Europe should play a more prominent role in advancing the well-being of its citizens in this context of globalisation, helping them anticipate and foster change" and prevent "a perception of insecurity, isolation, inequity and inequality."[46] The same document argues that it is "a matter of social justice and social cohesion" and an asset of "a modern and cohesive society" is "to allow everyone in the EU to have access to the resources, services, conditions and capabilities in order to turn the theoretical equality of opportunities and active citizenship into a meaningful reality."[47] Despite the apparent radicalism and novelty of this proposal, however, the document immediately proceeds by stressing: "This is an economic imperative. A well-functioning, confident and buoyant society which invests in its human capital and creates opportunities for individuals to move on throughout their life cycle is essential to sustain economic growth, labour market participation, living standards and combat social exclusion."[48]

The turn of the 2020s and the pandemic years of 2020 and 2021 brought about a powerful return of the term 'social cohesion' to the center of the EU policy discourse. The 2021 document, *Cohesion as an Overall Value of the European Union* advocates the idea of "bringing cohesion closer to the citizens and their well-being" and argues that this requires fundamentally rethinking cohesion and its purpose. As a result, the document proposes "a new Cohesion Spirit" to be embedded in all EU policies,[49] calling for shifting cohesion "from a 'flaking policy' to a policy objective in its own right"[50] and elevating it to "an overarching policy objective of the EU."[51]

Thus, while the specific term 'social cohesion' has moved in and out of prominence, and has been linked to a shifting array of other concepts—social capital, social inclusion, social investment, well-being, equality of opportunities—it is possible to point to several traits that have remained constant over the course of the three decades: The first two such traits relate to the broadly economic thrust of the policy: first, social cohesion is presented primarily as an economic imperative or a productive factor which contributes to the EU's sustainable economic growth and competitiveness; second, this means that policy focuses heavily on measures like active employment and the reinsertion of individuals and groups into the labor market. Thus, while cohesion appears as an antonym of exclusion, the necessary inclusion is primarily economic inclusion. The second pair of constant traits presents an apparent contradiction: despite the high priority of social cohesion in EU policy between 1990 and 2022, there is a little if any attempt to specify what social cohesion means and entails in the EU official documents; at the same time, however, the policy discourse includes a constant call for making the notion of social cohesion more operationalizable, which goes hand in hand with the policy proposal to put in place an effective monitoring, control and evaluation system to measure the progress in strengthening social cohesion through a scientifically grounded set of social cohesion indicators.

3.2 SOCIAL RIGHTS AND WELL-BEING OF ALL—SOCIAL COHESION POLICY OF THE COUNCIL OF EUROPE

The context in which the Council of Europe[52] introduces the notion of 'social cohesion' in its official policy documents around the mid-1990s is its effort to review the main trends in poverty and social exclusion across Europe. In its 1994 document, the council argues that "the real challenge facing Europe is certainly not military, and, in the long term, not even economic, but social: can the European social fabric continue to hold its citizens within it or, as is now more accurately the case, will increasing numbers fall from it? This is not a hypothetical situation but a real and growing one."[53] The council identifies several "interlocking factors of disintegration" of European society—such as chronic long-term unemployment, unrealistic expectations by people unaccustomed to economic challenge, family breakdowns, stark divisions in wealth and poverty, uneven and inappropriate educational achievements, or rising racism and xenophobia[54]—and suggests that all actors interested in promoting social justice in Europe should join their forces "in a concerted drive to consolidate social cohesion,"[55] supported by new instruments. These include initiating, commissioning and undertaking research on social cohesion; proposing activities to promote social cohesion; supporting the implementation of new social cohesion policies; and assessing the effectiveness of activities undertaken in the field of social cohesion.[56]

In 1997, the heads of state and government of the Council of Europe's forty member states declared that "social cohesion is one of the foremost needs of the wider Europe and should be pursued as an essential complement to the promotion of human rights and dignity"[57] and agreed that the council should intensify "its contribution to cohesion, stability and security in Europe."[58] The council clearly links the call for strengthening social cohesion to the enjoyment of fundamental human rights, which it sees as being threatened by manifestations of social exclusion such as persistent unemployment and poverty. In the council's view "social cohesion means promoting a Europe of social rights" and "enables the social link between the individual and society to be restored."[59] The council offers a long list of policy measures to be taken by the governments of member states as being the key instruments of social cohesion in Europe. These include, for example, giving social rights the same priority as that accorded to human rights; reforming existing social policies by basing them on the principle of solidarity, with the objective of apportioning aid to the most disadvantaged (young adults, women, children, old persons, single-parent families, large families, refugees and asylum seekers, members of ethnic minorities); promoting policies to prevent poverty;

stepping up policies for reintegration of marginalized or excluded persons; improving the process of participation and civil dialogue; and defining effective policies to fight unemployment.[60]

We can see that the most visible trait of the Council of Europe's social cohesion policy discourse is its focus on the question of social rights. The council advocates a rights-based approach to social cohesion which is centered around the idea of improving access to social rights for all members of society in the wider Europe. The notion of social cohesion seems to serve as a generic concept encompassing the entire realm of social rights. The council's approach connects social cohesion to the issue of social exclusion which it views as caused by poverty and unemployment and hindering the enjoyment of social rights of millions of members of European societies. Inclusion is therefore understood in terms of the extension of rights rather than as activation and incorporation into the labor market. Inadequate access to social rights is presented as a threat to social cohesion and, at the same time, as a threat to the very stability of European societies.

The Council of Europe entered the new millennium with its first comprehensive *Strategy for Social Cohesion*, prepared by the newly established European Committee for Social Cohesion. The *Strategy* deliberately avoids providing a precise definition of social cohesion, while characterizing it as "an ideal towards which societies have to strive continually" and "a goal to which they aspire, but never fully achieve."[61] It also offers a rich list of "factors of social cohesion" which represent the constituents of social cohesion, including strong social security systems, decent and adequately remunerated employment, support for families, citizens' aspirations toward greater solidarity and "sound economic policies that are not solely directed by market mechanisms."[62] What somewhat stands out from this list as a distinctive feature of the council's approach is the support for families, which are identified as central: "the family is a fundamental factor of social cohesion in the private domain; it can be described as the place where social cohesion is experienced and built."[63] Despite the obvious ideological assumptions this involves, this claim about the fundamental role of the family passes without justification and is simply presupposed as self-evident.

The *Strategy* also formulates a long list of 'goods' for which social cohesion is valuable. It views social cohesion as contributing to democratic security, social harmony, social peace, social stability in the long term, strengthened social solidarity and sense of belonging, promoting access to social rights, reducing the risk of social and political disruption, revitalizing economy, or a sound relationship between the state, the market and civil society.[64] A socially cohesive society is characterized as "conductive to the fulfilment of all its members"[65] and demonstrating the capacity to manage conflict and change constructively and creatively.[66] But the document is far from clear about the relationships between, or even the meaning of, the broad concepts it relies on, concepts such as 'social harmony,' 'social peace,' 'social stability,' 'social solidarity,' 'social rights,' and 'social cohesion.'

Whereas the 2000 *Strategy* eschewed any definition of social cohesion, the Council of Europe's 2004 *Revised Strategy* starts from a definition, one that relies on concepts not previously used in the Council's document related to social cohesion. It defines social cohesion as "the capacity of a society to ensure the welfare of all its members, minimising disparities and avoiding polarisation."[67] The *Revised Strategy* defends a rights-based account of the notion of 'welfare,' claiming that it implies "equity and non-discrimination in access to human rights," and also "the dignity of each person," "the freedom of each individual to pursue their personal development throughout their life" and "the possibility for each person to participate actively as a full member of society."[68] Thus the *Revised Strategy* emphasizes that social cohesion is more than a matter of curing the social ills of exclusion and poverty, but rather also a matter of creating solidarity in society such that social exclusion and poverty can be prevented. At the same time, the Council understands social cohesion as an ideal to be striven for, not as a goal that could ever be fully achieved by any real society. It is presented almost as a Kantian regulative ideal, an equivalent of a perfectly just society.

As for the actors responsible for promoting social cohesion, the *Revised Strategy* argues that "the capacity of a society to ensure the welfare of all must be seen as a responsibility for all sectors of society."[69] In particular, it argues that the state should maintain its essential role as a guarantor of human rights through mechanisms such as redistributive taxation and social security, protection of vulnerable groups at risk of social exclusion through providing social services, and so on—for reasons at least in part focused on the desirability of social cohesion. At the same time, the document recommends that we "move away from the omnicompetent State to new concepts of governance through partnership"[70] based on devolving responsibility to local authorities, members of civil society, businesses, media and other "social partners." This idea is closely related to the Council of Europe's basic assumption that "an exclusive stress on the rights of the individual cannot form a sufficient basis for social cohesion" and that "individual rights will be best protected in societies where people feel a shared responsibility for the rights and welfare of all."[71] In this context, the *Revised Strategy* invokes the role of participation of individuals in networks which "help to knit society together," such as charities, sports and cultural associations, arguing that such "socially useful voluntary activities" of individuals "play a particularly important part in building social cohesion."[72]

The Council of Europe calls for measuring the progress of social cohesion in member states by putting in practice a set of social cohesion indicators and creating an "observatory of social cohesion in Europe" with the task of collecting information and statistics on poverty and exclusion in the member states, and producing expert reports on questions relating to social cohesion as well as opinions on national and European policies to promote it.[73] The Council hopes that "the conceptual basis of the *Strategy for Social Cohesion* will be continually refined and extended so as to respond to new challenges and to integrate innovative methods and approaches."[74] True to its commitment to further developing the concept of social cohesion, the Council adopted a *New Strategy and Council of Europe Action Plan for Social Cohesion* in 2010. The *New Strategy* defines social cohesion as

> the capacity of a society to ensure the well-being of all its members—minimising disparities and avoiding marginalisation—to manage differences and divisions and ensure the means of achieving welfare for all members.[75]

The *New Strategy* thus conceives of the "well-being of all" as a shared goal in a cohesive society and stresses that achieving it requires "ensuring adequate resources are available to combat inequalities and exclusion."[76] But what precisely 'well-being' amounts to, and the precise relationship between the concepts of 'well-being' and 'welfare' remains far from clear in this document. Despite the Council of Europe's effort to develop a more precise definition of the notion, one of the council's own policy bodies critically noted that "the concept of social cohesion is fluid, perhaps too fluid and confused with social inclusion or participation."[77] However, the council has continued to use its 2010 definition of social cohesion and further develop the concept in the framework of ensuring equal and effective access to social rights.

The *New Strategy* also suggests that social cohesion is "a political concept" which refers to "a dynamic process" rather than a state of affairs.[78] Both remarks seem to draw on the Council of Europe's contention that "social cohesion cannot be imposed, nor achieved by following a one size fits all blueprint," but must be "adapted to specific situation in a country, region or municipality" even though all citizens should participate in defining the specific objectives and the pace of implementation of social cohesion policies.[79] As regards the question of who, or which institutions, should take responsibility for strengthening social cohesion, the *New Strategy* focuses primarily on the national-state level and considers "the fundamental responsibility of states and governments in terms of social cohesion" as undisputed.[80] Thus, "the responsibility for creating necessary conditions to promote and ensure social cohesion lies with the member states."[81] The basic assumption here is that the more socially cohesive the European nation states are, the more socially cohesive is Europe as a whole.[82] Yet, apart from identifying the states and governments as the key actors in promoting social cohesion, the document also puts a strong emphasis on the role of empowering citizens (including children, youth, elderly) to participate in elaborating common objectives and a shared vision in sensitive areas for future well-being. This bottom-up approach stresses the need to strengthen representation and democratic decision making, expand social dialogue and civic engagement, or foster social networks. However, the Council of Europe also expresses the awareness that "citizens' capacity for action depends to a large extent on political and institutional arrangements" and "without such arrangements, individuals—especially the most vulnerable—cannot fully accept responsibility for managing their own lives."[83]

Interestingly, the *New Strategy* avoids describing social cohesion as instrumental in the achievement of economic efficiency and progress, and indeed insists on the need thoroughly to examine "the social and environmental costs of current patterns of production and consumption."[84] It even calls for a "renewed vision of economic development" and "a new vision of security, based on non-material values that are indispensable for our well-being in the longer term, in particular social links and solidarity."[85]

Social cohesion, now unpacked in the ways we have seen, continues to maintain high priority as a policy objective of the Council of Europe in the early 2020s. In 2021, the council points out the "new challenges in social cohesion" which the COVID-19 pandemic posed for European societies and proudly contends that "there is no better venue for exploring the threats to and opportunities for social cohesion in a post-pandemic Europe" than in the Council of Europe as a pan-European organization with a long "history of work on social cohesion and on the protection of social rights."[86] In 2022, the Council of Europe replaced the European Social Cohesion Platform with the newly established European Committee for Social Cohesion. The official terms of reference for the period 2022–2025 instruct the committee to "ensure the mainstreaming of social cohesion throughout the Council of Europe by further developing the concept, by contributing to impact assessments of the various activities in the different sectors with regard to achieving social cohesion, including the relevant activities aimed at building inclusive societies, and by promoting specific actions which contribute to social cohesion."[87]

3.3 A COMPARISON AND CRITIQUE OF EUROPEAN SOCIAL COHESION POLICIES

We need first to take a closer look at key similarities and differences between the two main currents within which the notion of social cohesion was analyzed in the previous two sections. Both the European Union and the Council of Europe invoke narratives of threat and decline by referring to certain phenomena—such as permanent unemployment, endemic poverty, excessive disparities between various groups—as threats to social cohesion. They emphasize the magnitude of these threats by describing them as being at the same time threats to the stability of European society. Social cohesion is thus to be desired by all who value these things. Both organizations call for a more operationalizable concept of social cohesion which would allow for measurement, comparison, and assessment of progress in strengthening social cohesion. However, whenever a definition of social cohesion is made explicit (and often it is not, as we have seen) it always relies on other elastic and ambiguous notions such as that of well-being or of welfare. Both bodies conceive of social cohesion as closely related to—if not identical with—social inclusion as opposed to social exclusion, with the implicit threats understood less in terms of conflict between groups but certain groups being left out or left behind. Finally, and most importantly, the two organizations present social cohesion as both intrinsically valuable and as instrumental in respect of other goods and values such as the enjoyment of social rights, social justice, or economic growth.

The most striking difference between the EU and the Council of Europe's approaches concerns the relationship of social cohesion to the question of rights. The Council of Europe conceives of social cohesion as a matter of equal access to social rights with reference to the European Social Charter, whereas the EU almost entirely avoids rights-based discourse and links social cohesion primarily to the question of equal opportunities and inclusion in the labor market. Thus, the framing of social cohesion as a matter of social inclusion has a radically different meaning for the two organizations. In terms of content the EU thus focuses on labor market measures, whereas the Council of Europe focuses on a broad spectrum of social policies around housing, health care, education, culture, and/or civic participation. These differences surface in their conceptions of the fundamental value of social cohesion: the EU conceives of it as inseparable from its contribution to economic growth and competitiveness in the global market, whereas the Council of Europe's rights-based approach rather decouples it from its contribution to economic progress, stressing that social cohesion must not be put at risk for the goal of economic growth.

When it comes to the EU, the close association between social cohesion and economic growth, competitiveness, and the idea of 'active solidarity' in the form of incorporation into the labor market is ripe for criticism. It is hardly a stretch to suggest that this reflects strongly neoliberal trends towards the economization of the social and the assumption that enhancing competitiveness is a core goal at the level of both society and the individual.[88] This chimes with the tendency identified by Dobbernack for "the imperative of socio-economic activity that was characteristic for 'back to work' objectives [to be] conjoined with ideals of civicness or social contact."[89] In such a framing, encouraging participation becomes elevated to a goal, while the form of cooperation becomes narrowed to economic participation, with citizens represented as bearers of human capital. Moreover, when the EU brings social cohesion into the orbit of other concepts, it tends to repeat this economizing logic. Thus, while lip service is paid to the idea of social capital's negative effects, in practice promoting social capital is represented as a positive thing that contributes to cohesion. The assumption remains that the more connections that are built, the more people are engaged and moved into activity, the better the society will be. Thus, as with some of the theories we criticized in the previous chapter, the *quantity* of social interactions and participation appears to be more important than their *quality*. This parallels Fine's description of the policy perspective of social capital as "self-help raised to the level of the collective" which "offers the golden opportunity of improving the status quo without challenging it."[90] Similarly, the shift to connecting social cohesion to social investment after the financial crisis continued to reproduce a neoliberal logic based on enhancing and activating human capital and "the application of the economic rationale and the cost–benefit logic to all domains of society."[91] The identification of inclusion with activation also tends to reduce citizens to economic subjects that need to be motivated and activated, occluding more meaningful forms of democratic inclusion: "Activated subjects, captured in a network of measures and initiatives, find themselves pushed towards ideals they had no voice in shaping."[92] This only becomes more pernicious when the 'excluded' become identified with specific groups within society (for example the disabled, or certain ethnic minorities), and the activation policies become more disciplinary (for example through policies of 'workfare').[93]

Of course, the significantly more expansive vision of the Council of Europe shows that 'social cohesion' need not be reduced and subordinated to economic concerns. Though there are certainly traces of the logic of 'activation' in the council's emphasis on encouraging volunteering and personal responsibility, they are clearly linked to a richer sense of democratic participation. However, the very fact that 'social cohesion' can be put to service in such apparently conflicting visions should give serious pause for thought. Not only do we see the concept used in the service of competing political agendas, but there is also a great deal of ambiguity and unclarity within them. This is repeatedly recognized by the institutions themselves but is treated as a problem that is resolvable through the development of a more operationalizable and robust concept. However, it turns out that the resulting definitions are *themselves* vague and ambiguous: they depend on concepts that themselves require further unpacking and specification. Thus, the Council of Europe can develop a definition that incorporates 'welfare' *and* 'well-being' *and* 'marginalisation' *and* 'reducing disparities,' recognize that this definition is vague, but continue to use it. Seen in this light, 'social cohesion' increasingly appears to have the status of what the editors Cornwall and Eade describe as "buzzwords and fuzzwords."[94] These are concepts that are frequently invoked by agencies, governments, and commentators, as if their meaning were clear and uncontroversial—when in fact it is not—and whose actual use thus tends to obscure and mislead. As Deborah Eade stresses, "a buzzword will have a multitude of meanings and nuances, depending on who is using it and in what context." Such terms "appear to convey one thing but are in practice used to mean something quite different, or . . . indeed have no real meaning at all."[95]

The importance of this lies in the fact that one way in which such concepts function is to elicit broad agreement where with greater clarity and precision there might well be substantive disagreement. As Standing puts it with regard to the concept of social protection, "A statement such as 'we must devote more resources to social protection' might elicit consensus support and nods of agreement. But few might agree if what the speaker meant was that more resources should be devoted to workfare schemes, or conversely to give every citizen a basic income without obligations."[96] Thus, as we have seen, while the Council of Europe and the European Union have two very different understandings of social inclusion—which imply very different policy responses—both are nevertheless happy to incorporate them into the language of social cohesion. When removed from these contexts, and treated as a singular concept, it thus blurs together different ideological commitments and projects. Persistent vagueness both reflects and reinforces this blurring, suggesting that, as Maloutas and Malouta argue, "The vagueness of the concept is not due to poor or contradictory academic work, but to the fact that its content is the subject of multiple *rapport des forces* between social groups and political organizations that are trying to impose their own project of social cohesion."[97]

In this context, the emergence of the notion of social cohesion in the 1990s—frequently understood at the time in terms of the 'end of history' and the obsolescence of traditional ideologies—is particularly significant. Social cohesion appears as a way for both the EU and the Council of Europe to link various social ills and grievances into a clear narrative and put a name to a sense of crisis. Various policies, desirable or not, gain an additional layer of legitimacy from the rhetorical power of the narrative of threat. Even the Council of Europe's more expansive rights-based vision frames those rights as much as an antidote to the risk of disintegration as either a matter of social justice or the disadvantage of the excluded. In both cases, then, threats to social cohesion give a clear reason for government action that does not depend on any preexisting ideological commitments, but only the apparently uncontroversial idea that society ought to hold together—indeed, the stress on *inclusion* seems to suggest that the most appropriate social form has already been identified and it is simply a matter of making sure that everyone fits in. Thus, social cohesion provides a rationale for social policy to shape behavior in a context where the government might otherwise be committed to pluralism or liberal neutrality concerning the good life. As Dobbernack observes, "The protection of community, the strengthening of social capital or the preservation of social cohesion all offer reasons for social governance that, at least occasionally, is prescriptive of attitudes and conduct beyond the limitations of liberal non-interference."[98] While the government's imposition of substantive values on societies has become increasingly suspect, the idea that they might intervene to secure 'cohesion' seems less so. The Council of Europe, for example, is able to elevate a 'cohesive society' to the level of a regulative ideal in part because it appears as an uncontroversial goal in a way that a 'good' or 'just' society does not.

This is particularly significant given that social cohesion is variously represented as both a valuable goal in itself and instrumentally valuable for a growing shopping list of different goods. Here we can see the risks of normative overdetermination pointed to in chapter 2 in their full effect. In short, the different sources and levels of normativity in the concept of social cohesion crisscross and combine with each other in a way that obscures their relationship and inflates and expands its significance. Moreover, the repeated emphasis on social cohesion's obvious goodness contributes all too easily to its naturalization and reification, insofar as it is "no longer considered a social construct or the result of political will, but rather the consequence of a 'natural' world order that was deemed just and desirable."[99] The more that 'social cohesion' comes to represent something necessarily good and naturally desirable, the harder it is to resist policies carried out in its name. Eade argues that, like toxic substances, such 'fuzzwords' can "serve to numb the critical faculties of those who end up using them, wrapping up all manner of barbed policies and practices in linguistic cotton wool."[100] Thus, although many such concepts might well have been originally conceived as part of a counter-hegemonic approach to radical social transformation (compare 'participation' or 'citizenship') they have become "consensual hurrah-words" which "gain their purchase and power through their vague and euphemistic qualities, their capacity to embrace a multitude of possible meanings, and their normative resonance."[101] Through the extensive use of these concepts in the mainstream policy discourse and the "subterranean process of challenging and subverting the politics that the term was created to symbolise," they became flattened, depoliticized and deprived of their former contestability. In this context, the repeated demand for a more measurable and operationalizable concept simply serves to push the concept further from contestation: 'If only we can work out what it is and how to measure it, we can finally stop debating and get on with putting it into practice.'

3.4 CONCLUSION

Let us sum up. Social cohesion emerges as a significant concept in the 1990s in the discourse of both the European Union and the Council of Europe. While both institutions frame the need for social cohesion policies in terms of threats related to changing economic and social conditions, first and foremost social exclusion, they conceive of the policies required to address this very differently. While the Council of Europe links social cohesion to a vision of a just society and a broad set of social rights, and at least opens up the possibility that social cohesion might be in conflict with economic growth and efficiency, the European Union sees the value of social cohesion primarily as a lever for economic growth, and thus sees inclusion as primarily a matter of labor market incorporation.

The very fact that 'social cohesion' can be used in the service of two quite different ideological projects indicates its flexibility and ambiguity. While this ambiguity is sometimes recognized, it does not seem to have led to any doubts about the concept itself. Rather, the concept thrives in part *because* of this ambiguity, allowing different agendas to be bound together and shielded from criticism. In this way, invocations of social cohesion risk at best conserving the *status quo* and at worst giving cover to more pernicious ideological agendas.

Chapter 4

Exporting Cohesive Societies
Social Cohesion and International Development

The previous chapter discussed the development of social cohesion policy frameworks at the European level. In this chapter, we will move beyond the European context and take a closer look at social cohesion policies and programs formulated in the global context of international development, in particular the Organisation for Economic Co-operation and Development (OECD) and the United Nations (UN). In several respects, the criticisms of this chapter mirror those of the previous one. We will see the same combination of demands for measurement and clarity with a multiplication of definitions, as well as the tendency to elevate 'social cohesion' to an ideal or goal, increasingly linked to other values and concepts. However, the shift to the international development context also adds an additional set of problems, as 'social cohesion' becomes increasingly linked to fixed and narrow models of development or progress that often appear as outside impositions on developing nations. While many of these criticisms apply to development discourse in general, social cohesion seems to slide easily into these discourses in a way that reproduces these same problems.

Before leaving Europe, however, it is worth noting that—unsurprisingly—both the European Union and the Council of Europe constructed their international development initiatives around the concept of social cohesion. The Council of Europe, for example, at its "Conference on Euro-Mediterranean Partnership for Social Cohesion and Social Development" (Alexandria, 2002) secured agreement regarding the importance of refocusing from "internal social cohesion within Europe" to "world social cohesion"[1] and to consider how European ideas about social cohesion impact policies in countries outside Europe, in particular in the Global South. European and non-European countries alike were encouraged to "achieve policy coherence across all government departments . . . to consolidate fragmented social policies in a strong national strategy aimed at poverty eradication and reinforcing social cohesion."[2] The European Union began to cooperate on social cohesion with the Latin American and Caribbean region as early as 2002, resulting in the 2004 *Declaration of Guadalajara*. Its signatories—heads of state in Latin America, the Caribbean, and the EU (including the ten member states that joined in 2004)—declare that bearing in mind the principle of "global common responsibility,"[3] they are determined to "build fairer societies by strengthening social cohesion."[4] They commit themselves to "prioritise social cohesion as one of the main elements of our bi-regional strategic partnership"[5] and to "recognise the importance of integrating the social cohesion dimension into national strategies and development processes."[6]

This begins to give a sense of the variety of international institutions, agencies, and agreements that began to see themselves as promoting social cohesion in the early years of this century. Since then, there has been a veritable explosion of reliance on 'social cohesion' by NGOs, international financial institutions, national development agencies, and private or charitable organizations.[7] Focusing primarily on the OECD and the UN[8] is partly for reasons of space, but also because they represent two of the largest and most influential international bodies, with strong mandates and a substantial membership. While they differ from each other in significant ways,[9] they also differ significantly from single-country based, nongovernmental, banking or think-tank types of organization.[10] While this inevitably narrows the scope of our treatment, it allows us to trace clear lines of evolution in international development thinking. It is also worth noting at the outset that while most of the policy documents in the previous chapter were formally adopted by the institutions as collective positions, most of the documents in this chapter are published by the institutions but authored by named individuals, usually a research group employed directly or commissioned by the agency concerned. This often means that the analysis goes somewhat deeper, giving more scope for individual researchers; at the same time, it pulls the documents away from being the responsibility of the institution as a whole—indeed they are often accompanied by a disclaimer to precisely that.

4.1 CONNECTING ECONOMIC GROWTH AND HUMAN DEVELOPMENT—SOCIAL COHESION IN THE OECD

The Organisation for Economic Co-operation and Development (OECD) was formed in 1961, following the reform of the Organisation for European Economic Co-operation, with a remit to administer funds from the Marshall Plan. Its founding members consisted of Western European countries plus

Turkey and the United States. Since 1989 it has expanded several times to incorporate thirty-eight full member states. Its members are primarily high-income countries and are committed to market economy and democratic governance, although its development programs operate across the world.

The language of social cohesion begins to appear in the OECD in 1996 when, strongly mirroring contemporaneous EU discourse, its secretariat began to question the sustainability of welfare systems in its member countries: "In most countries these systems have become unstable for reasons ranging from purely demographic changes to changes in the composition of employment . . . , leading to a loss of social cohesion and even, in some countries, of consensus on the desirability of the systems themselves."[11] To address this, the secretariat held a high-level conference, "Beyond 2000: The New Social Policy Agenda" in Paris in November 1996. It stressed that "high and persistent unemployment puts strong pressures on social spending and threatens social cohesion"[12] and identified as a key social policy the objective of ensuring "full participation in society and economic life."[13] They also agreed that the right policy approach to be adopted in OECD countries was the 'social investment' approach: "The challenge is to ensure that the returns to social expenditures are maximised, in the form of social cohesion and active participation in society and the labour market. This approach stresses interventions that take place early in the life-cycle or that support those contributing to their own welfare."[14]

The following month, a further conference was held, aiming to "stimulate innovative thinking about ways to maintain future societal cohesion in the face of a dynamic economy that thrives on a high degree of flexibility."[15] Its main concern was "the long-run compatibility of economic flexibility with sustainable societal cohesion in OECD countries,"[16] a discourse characterized by a dual, perhaps even circular, sense of threat: economic reforms are necessary to address the risks to cohesion brought about by failures of the welfare state; but at the same time, the economic flexibility necessary to deal with those failures presents a *new* threat to social cohesion. Thus the conference summary points to "a growing political disenchantment arising from the increasing income polarisation, persistently high levels of unemployment, and widespread social exclusion that are manifesting themselves in varying ways across North America, Europe and OECD Pacific,"[17] while the OECD secretariat itself concomitantly claims that "problems of social exclusion and a growing sense of insecurity are manifest in virtually all OECD countries" and that "the diffusion of this malaise throughout society threatens to undermine both the drive towards greater economic flexibility and the policies that encourage strong competition, globalisation, and technological innovation."[18]

Nonetheless, the report assures its readers that a solution to these threats is readily available:

Of course, competition and structural change are not fundamentally incompatible with societal cohesion. On the contrary, they are a motor of the economic growth and prosperity on which cohesion can thrive. Reciprocally, a strong social fabric provides a secure basis for the flexibility and risk-taking which are the lifeblood of vibrant economic activity and wealth creation. Striking sustainable balance between dynamism and security constitute one of the primary missions of the political process. The capacity to find the appropriate balance, thereby avoiding both stagnation and social fragmentation, is one of the key strengths of OECD democracies.[19]

The document envisions two alternative scenarios of how "the mechanism of societal cohesion might evolve in OECD countries over the coming decades."[20] While in what they call 'individualistic scenario' the society does the utmost to encourage individual freedom and responsibility, radically reducing the role of governments in all domains, offering greater flexibility in the allocation of resources by individuals and firms, in the 'solidaristic scenario' much greater emphasis is put on collective organizations, particularly public institutions, universal rights and redistributive frameworks as ways of hedging risks. Suggesting a degree of pluralism and openness, the OECD maintains that the two scenarios "underscore the wide range of possible outcomes for OECD societies," stressing the importance of the political process for the future development of social cohesion in the OECD countries, and blithely assuming that "the actual contours of future societies will be shaped in part, by values as determined by history, institutions and culture, and expressed through political choices."[21] Thus the OECD recommends enhancing the democratic infrastructure of OECD societies, in particular putting "greater emphasis on the renewal of decision-making and participatory processes" and on improving "systems of governance."[22]

Despite this apparent openness, however, the OECD eventually recommends "a less dominant role for government in securing societal cohesion in the context of a comprehensive strategy based on the extension of universal rights and the pursuit of policies that offer individuals great choice and self-determination."[23] Central to this, clearly, is a sense that economic growth is a minimum requirement; the document concludes that "conference participants generally agreed that the wide range of challenges to societal cohesion in OECD countries are unlikely to be resolved by the dividends arising from modest economic growth."[24] While "weaker growth could bring with it the risk of social strife and a disintegration of the economic policy consensus," "stronger growth rates might ease somewhat the pressures to adapt and at the same time provide greater room to manoeuvre."[25]

However, there is a substantial shift in the OECD's thinking about social cohesion at the beginning of the 2010s. Although not explicitly claimed as such, it is plausible to suggest that this shift was shaped by the 2008 financial crisis and the growing critique of narrow, economic accounts of development. Thus, *The Well-Being of Nations: The Role of Human and Social Capital*, published in 2011, broadens the picture by introducing and emphasizing the notion of "human well-being." Following Amartya Sen's account of "human capabilities,"[26] the report argues that human well-being "includes economic well-being but also extends to the enjoyment of civil liberties, relative freedom from crime, enjoyment of a clean environment and individual states of mental and physical health."[27] Here the OECD seems to adopt the view that economic well-being is just one component of human well-being among other important components such as realization of opportunities for individuals to choose and achieve life goals that best suit them, which in turn requires a viable social and natural environment. These 'insights' lay the ground in particular for its new understanding of 'sustainable development,' a notion which "has now acquired a broader meaning, implying that the objectives of increasing economic efficiency and material wealth must take into account social and environmental concerns within an overall policy framework."[28] On this basis, the document eventually settles on Jane Jenson's proposal for conceptualizing social cohesion as comprising five essential dimensions: belonging, inclusion, participation, recognition, and legitimacy.[29] The distinction between social cohesion and social capital is then more clearly elaborated in the OECD's *Perspectives on Global Development 2012: Social Cohesion in a Shifting World*, which asserts (in line with most of the accounts discussed in chapter 2) that "social cohesion is a more holistic concept extended to the level of the entire society."[30] Significantly, this document provides what became the standard OECD definition, that "a society is 'cohesive' if it works towards the well-being of all its members, fights exclusion and marginalisation, creates a sense of belonging, promotes trust, and offers its members the opportunity of upward social mobility"[31]—adding that "a cohesive society is one where citizens feel they can trust their neighbours and state institutions . . . one where individuals can seize opportunities for improving their own well-being and the well-being of their children . . . a society where individuals feel protected when facing illness, unemployment or old age."[32]

As we have seen, this view of social cohesion is self-consciously distinguished from a narrower view which conceives the bonding nature of networks and institutions as the core of social cohesion. This report also explicitly links its broader view to the Rawlsian notion of a 'well-ordered society' in which, regardless of conflicting religious or personal beliefs, an overlapping consensus would be possible as long as members of society were open to compromise.[33] It thus distinguishes three dimensions of social cohesion: (1) social inclusion—measured by elements such as poverty, inequality, and social polarization; (2) social capital—combining interpersonal and societal trust and various forms of civic engagement; and (3) social mobility—the degree to which people can, or believe they can, change their position in society.[34] The OECD then proposes four variables whereby to measure social cohesion: (1) income inequality; (2) the unemployment rate as a "thermometer for monitoring levels of life satisfaction and the risk of civil tensions";[35] (3) "subjective well-being measures"[36] such as life expectancy, literacy rates, instruments supporting wider participation in civil society and political life, and high-quality formal institutions (clearly based on the Stiglitz-Sen-Fitoussi Commission's report[37]); and (4) social capital, for example, group membership, interpersonal trust.

This view of social cohesion is closely linked to the idea of progress: "social cohesion and its components can themselves be considered dimensions of social progress," so that "better understanding social cohesion can, therefore, also help to better understand how to measure society's progress."[38] Thus the OECD claims that "social cohesion is a valuable goal in itself."[39] However, the document at the same time maintains that "social cohesion and the absence of socially divisive influences contribute to desirable development outcomes such as growth, poverty reduction, stability, peace, and conflict resolution. What is more, social cohesion helps make policies more effective."[40] Finally, the OECD contends that there is a "mutually beneficial interplay between social cohesion, growth and development"[41] and that social cohesion "contributes to maintaining long-term economic growth."[42] Social cohesion, then, is "both a means to development and an end in itself."[43]

The tension inherent in this claim unsurprisingly gives rise to a more nervous sense of threat. Thus the 2012 report endorses the Club of Madrid's claim that "if sections of society are marginalised they will contribute less to the economy. . . . They have less capital to invest. . . . They may go farther and resist the *status quo* and it may cost the state a good deal of its surplus wealth to maintain the *status quo*. The state may resort to increased security measures, such as enlarged security forces, enhanced equipment for the security services, larger and stronger prisons."[44] What this appears to amount to is that social cohesion is desirable because governing a 'cohesive society' is easier and cheaper than governing a society replete with marginalized groups. In this vein, the OECD report goes on to warn that "governments who ignore the broader questions of inclusion and social cohesion do so at the peril of social instability, ineffective policy interventions and, ultimately, a possible loss of political power."[45] In light of this sense of economic threat, it is notable that part II of *Perspectives on Global Development* includes a proposal for policy recommendations (in the field of employment, education, social protection) and stresses how "the structural transformation of economies brought about by integration into the world economy offers various unprecedented possibilities to foster social cohesion."[46] Similarly, a 2014 *Social Cohesion Policy*

Review of Viet Nam stresses how "sustained and inclusive economic growth needs to remain high on the policy agenda. . . . Growth strategies also need stronger linkages with employment-friendly policies."[47] These recommendations can be placed within a broader context of critiques of conditionality, such that aid and assistance tend to come with conditions based on economic and social reform—for all the broader and high-minded emphasis on capacities and well-being, economic 'reform' remains a necessary condition. While the OECD does not have the power to enforce or sanction its members, it has adopted strategies of "peer review and peer pressure,"[48] which have rightly been criticized in terms of creating a democratic deficit,[49] for instance by Duncan Green of Oxfam: "the danger is that instead of looking afresh at what it contributes to our understanding of development, we just recycle our existing set of ideas and say 'because of complexity/ social cohesion/ climate change, you should do exactly what we've been saying all along.'"[50]

4.2 MULTIPLYING DEFINITIONS AND LOCAL SENSITIVITIES—SOCIAL COHESION AND THE UNITED NATIONS

Perhaps surprisingly, the United Nations comes relatively late to the social cohesion party. Its uses of the term emerge across various regional documents rather than at the level of, for example, the General Assembly. Indeed, although some documents suggest that social cohesion is at the heart of the influential UN 2030 Agenda, the term itself does not appear at all in any of its seventeen development goals. One of the first regional documents to focus on social cohesion was prepared by the UN's Economic Commission for Latin America and the Caribbean (ECLAC) for the seventeenth Ibero-American Summit of Heads of State and Government in Chile in 2007 on the theme of "Social Cohesion and Social Policies for More Inclusive Societies in Ibero-America."[51] The background is a sense that the "perception of social injustice, combined with unfulfilled expectations of social mobility and access to resources and consumption, erodes confidence in the system, weakens the legitimacy of democracy and exacerbates conflicts";[52] and so ECLAC argues that "the importance of social cohesion for the stable functioning of society, particularly in Latin America, and, above all, for the consolidation and improvement of democratic institutions cannot be overemphasized."[53]

The ECLAC document is striking in its level of detail and sophistication when it comes to recognizing both the breadth of the "the 'semantic universe' of social cohesion"[54] and in defining it as "the dialectic between instituted social inclusion and exclusion mechanisms and the responses, perceptions and attitudes of citizens towards the way these mechanisms operate."[55] This understanding of inclusion is significantly more expansive than merely economic or labor market incorporation, stressing in particular the "positive relationship between the full exercise of citizenship and social cohesion, inasmuch as the former includes, or is intended to include, rights that combine the political (participation, deliberation, a voice) with the social (access to goods, income, services) and the communicational (culture, identity, visibility)."[56] In terms of policy, this is divided into three pillars: (1) the growth of opportunities in the productive economy; (2) the development of individual capabilities; and (3) the establishment of more inclusive safety nets to deal with vulnerability and risk.[57] It is the last of these that receives the most attention, framed in the context of the failure of both "a partial welfare-State model derived from the notion of a 'labour-based society'" and "the pro-market reforms of the 1990s" which only entrenched inequality further.[58] Thus

> If it is to have a positive and lasting influence on social cohesion, universal rights-based social protection cannot be limited to welfare or relief measures. It also has to encompass policies for the development of human capital and risk prevention for all.... This calls for anticipatory and remedial social investment measures to strengthen human and social capital, employment-based social security schemes that reflect the heterogeneity of working conditions, and social protection or safety nets when these are absent.[59]

While some of this chimes in with the OECD's emphasis on the importance of human capital, it also clearly goes beyond it to recognize both the importance of various social protections and rights and active participation. This is framed in terms of a "social cohesion contract" that must be "supported by a wide range of agents"[60] to "create an understanding of the role and duties of the State and of members of society in relation to the attainment of democratic social cohesion, and to call them to account for the performance of these duties."[61] This socially cohesive contract must in turn be "based on the plurality of social identities and the recognition that no one identity must be allowed to obliterate the importance of others."[62]

ECLAC was not the only UN agency discussing social cohesion fifteen years ago. The United Nations Development Programme (UNDP)—whose mandate is to "end poverty, build democratic governance, rule of law, and inclusive institutions"[63]—offered its first conceptualization of social cohesion in *Community Security and Social Cohesion: Towards a UNDP Approach* (2009). This document describes social cohesion as "an elusive concept—easier to recognize by its absence than by any definition,"[64] an absence that results "in increased social tension, violent crime, targeting of minorities, human rights violations, and, ultimately, violent conflict."[65] Despite initially proposing a focus on the absence of social cohesion, however, and admitting that "the meaning of social cohesion is contested," the UNDP proceeds to draw heavily on the account of social cohesion developed by Berger-Schmitt for the EU.[66] It claims that "there are two principal dimensions to it: the reduction of disparities, inequalities and social exclusion; the strengthening of social relations, interactions and ties";[67] and extend this to add that "social cohesion is about tolerance of, and respect for, diversity (in terms of religion, ethnicity, economic situation, political preferences, sexuality, gender and age)—both institutionally and individually."[68]

Despite the effort to develop this account in 2009, it is strikingly *not* used in the UNDP's specific regional projects. A report of the regional project, "Promoting Social Cohesion in the Arab Region (PSCAR),"[69] admits that "the concept of social cohesion remains a fluid one" and "utilizing this concept to build a unifying agenda requires investment in analytical work that would guide the ensuing advocacy initiatives and technical support."[70] Rather than building on the 2009 document, this document draws on an account of social cohesion divided into four dimensions that is almost identical to Jenson's 1998 account.[71] The aim of the project thus becomes, quite familiarly, "to promote social cohesion, with a focus on equal citizenship, trust among citizens as well as between citizen and state; and pluralistic acceptance of the other, of different faiths, confessions, ethnic backgrounds, and political ideologies."[72] The representatives of Arab governments, civil society, academia, and think tanks that participated in the consultation meeting in Amman in 2014 apparently "confirmed that social cohesion is a priority for the region" and "also endorsed the definition provided and the framework proposed in the consultation's concept note."[73] But they also called for "a methodology/index to measure social cohesion and monitor its development across time," which would help "better define and contextualize this concept, which may be defined differently by different individuals, groups."[74] Charles Harb, professor of political and social psychology at the American University of Beirut, was commissioned to lead this process, with its results presented in *Developing a Social Cohesion Index for the Arab Region* (2017), which pursues an approach close to that of Chan et al. discussed in chapter 2.[75]

This attempt at measurement was repeated in two other UNDP projects: a project in Cyprus, co-funded by the American development organization USAID, *Predicting Peace: The Social Cohesion and Reconciliation Index as a Tool for Conflict Transformation* (2015); and *Towards a Measurement of Social Cohesion for Africa* (2016). Both documents express a certain ambivalence towards the concept of social cohesion: The former calls it an abstract theoretical construct or a "multi-dimensional 'umbrella' construct,"[76] while the latter describes it as "a nebulous concept"[77] and complains that while the "qualities and advantages" of social cohesion "appear evident and clear in theory, its conceptual ambiguity also presents a challenge to applied research."[78] Nonetheless, these concerns are overcome and both proceed to offer ways of measuring social cohesion. The document on Cyprus proposes three key indicators, including "trust in institutions, human security, and satisfaction with civic life."[79] Of these, human security is the main focus, understood as "an antecedent, as well as a consequence of, the other components constituting social cohesion" and described analogously to job security: "Human security can predict satisfaction with personal life, in the same way that job security can predict feelings of job satisfaction."[80] The document on Africa adopts the 2009 dimensions of reducing disparities and exclusion and strengthening social relations, and proposes that the new measure of social cohesion for Africa should consist of six main dimensions: inclusion, belonging, social relationships, participation, legitimacy, and security.[81] Adding to this already fragmented picture, in 2020 the UNDP published *Strengthening Social Cohesion: Conceptual Framing and Programming Implications*. This approaches cohesion as "the extent of trust in government and within society and the willingness to participate collectively toward a shared vision of sustainable peace and common development goals."[82] However, a footnote to the definition warns that "this definition does not connote a formal UNDP definition of the term social cohesion."[83] Moreover, yet another definition of social cohesion appears in the document in a chapter on conflict dynamics and peacebuilding: "Social cohesion is a product of networks and connections based on trust and interaction that can address or ameliorate root causes or prevent escalation. Such conceptualization informs a framework of analysis for social cohesion that can help to improve conflict vulnerability assessment frameworks."[84]

What is clear from all this is that, despite the repeated desire for a measurable and comparable account of social cohesion, what we see instead is a multiplication of different, overlapping framings and indicators. To the extent that there is any convergence at all, it seems to be around the broad framing identified by Chan et al. in terms of horizontal/vertical and subjective/objective dimensions of social cohesion. Thus, the 2020 document argues, "In UNDP-related practice, social cohesion may be described along two main dimensions: vertical and horizontal. Both include objective and subjective aspects. The horizontal dimension may also be described in terms of bonding, bridging and linking social capital. The vertical dimension represents trust between government and society."[85] This is perhaps particularly ironic, since Chan et al. explicitly *reject* that social cohesion might be understood as a "process" with an "end-state" or "maximal level" of social cohesion.[86] Yet the underlying logic suggests that social cohesion is something to be achieved, or at least strived for, in a maximizing way. While the 2007 ECLAC document had claimed that "while social cohesion is not a panacea, and it is not being suggested here that it can be fully realized, it is an essential part of a systemic approach to development,"[87] a 2015 report on a social cohesion project in Myanmar nonetheless insists that "social cohesion is not an ideal, but rather an attainable objective requiring the active and constant commitment of all levels of society."[88]

One reason for the shifting pattern of indicators and dimensions in all these documents is the desire to adapt to local circumstances. Thus the Myanmar document stresses that "social cohesion is context-specific; and so generic indicators have to be adapted and data has to be disaggregated as the situation demands,"[89] while local stakeholders in the Arab region stressed the importance of an index in part to "better define and contextualize this concept, which may be defined differently by different individuals, groups."[90] The document on the Arab region notes how local representatives and stakeholders pointed out an issue of "forced cohesion" during the colonial era, suggesting perhaps a sensitivity to particular models of social cohesion being imposed from outside, whereas the UNDP suggests that "Unity in those countries, rather than cohesion, was maintained by force, either by the colonial powers and, later, by strong military men."[91] The assumption here is that locals should not worry, because whatever *that* was, it could not have been *cohesion*.

4.3 SOCIAL COHESION AND INTERNATIONAL DEVELOPMENT—A CRITIQUE

The usage of notions of social cohesion in the international development context mirrors several of the trends outlined in the earlier chapters. In the late 1990s, and in the OECD in particular, it emerged in response to a perceived crisis brought on by the failures of the welfare state and the need for new forms of 'economic flexibility.' At this stage it is broadly defined in terms of 'social fabric' and grasped primarily in terms of employment policies. By the 2010s, however, it has undergone a notable thickening, incorporating broader notions of well-being and sustainability and an emphasis on a broader range of human capacities. It thus develops from a term describing an underlying structure of society in need of maintenance and repair to a goal or ideal to be achieved, not least as it was adopted—in however muddled a way—by UN agencies. In short, once social cohesion comes to be framed as something to be *achieved* and worked *towards*, both organizations emphasize the need for metrics of measurement that make it possible to track progress, and to that end adopt universalist definitions. This drive towards universalism is even more starkly visible in some of the other international development agencies. For example, Leininger et al.'s *Social Cohesion: A New Definition and a*

Proposal for Its Measurement in Africa, produced for the German Institute of Development and Sustainability, laments that "no consistent, temporally and geographically spread-out data on the different elements of social cohesion exists that would allow for a global analysis of social cohesion," insisting that the "rather fragmented picture of analytical approaches calls for a more universal definition and measurement of social cohesion" which "travels across regions and countries."[92]

Unsurprisingly then, many of the criticisms we have developed in previous chapters also apply here. Despite the desire for measurable and operationalizable accounts, there seems to be little convergence on any single account—most starkly illustrated by the UNDP's failure to settle on a definition even across its own different projects. As with previous accounts, the problem here is not that they fail to *provide* a unitary definition, but that they insist on the need for one while in fact merely multiplying different ones. Similarly, the gradual thickening of the notion repeats the process of 'normative overdetermination' we discussed earlier, where social cohesion is multiply defined as minimally and uncontroversially necessary for society to exist (as a 'social fabric'); instrumentally valuable for other specific goods; and incorporating a number of other important values. In both cases, we are presented with a veneer of scientific and normative legitimacy, a crucial component of which is its limiting space for criticism and contestation.

At the same time, the shift to the international development context adds several dimensions to this process. The fact that these documents have named authors and involve an institutional disavowal raises more directly the question of the relationship between science and policy. As we have stressed, in some places (most notably the ECLAC documents), this gives scientists freer rein to develop more sophisticated and critical accounts beyond the constraints of existing organizational policies and political agendas. At the same time, it raises challenging questions regarding the limits of this freedom:

> Some global institutions are by no means indifferent in this respect but are keen to coach research in particular directions on a grand scale, using the power of the purse and their sway over member government departments to orchestrate research efforts into broad programmatic strategies. With key questions, concepts and at times methodologies pre-cooked and already reflecting particular ways of looking at problems, the room for independent researchers following their own idiosyncratic inclinations and agenda and occasionally producing original vistas of the issues at stake, risks getting smothered and eclipsed.[93]

With some exceptions, the documents analyzed rarely present novel or surprising perspectives that challenge the mainstream: research on social cohesion tends to be seen as complementary to existing strategies, agendas, and interests of policymaking institutions, and as building on a secure basis of preexisting science.

Even more significantly, though, the context of development tightens the connection between social cohesion and progress. As social cohesion shifts from background fabric to goal or ideal, it fits neatly into understandings of development as proceeding indefinitely according to a specific and predetermined pattern. This idea has been subjected to trenchant critique as inscribed in the very core of the Western imaginary and seeking to distinguish Western culture from all others.[94] This of course often involves the imposition of such ideals in a distinctively paternalistic manner:

> Development embodies an urge to protect and better others less fortunate than ourselves. As such, it indicates a noble and emancipatory aspiration. Development, however, transforms this urge into a liberal will to govern through the assertion of an educative trusteeship over life that is always experienced as somehow incomplete and consequently surplus or in excess of prevailing requirements.[95]

This chimes with Juan Telleria's criticism of the UNDP itself, which suggests that it "tackles the 21st century global society using sociological assumptions of the colonial, Victorian 19th century."[96] Telleria argues that UNDP discourse adopts an essentialist standpoint based on "specific essential anthropological and sociological foundations [that] sustain and govern its discourse—which are assumed, yet not demonstrated."[97] These assumptions include the conviction that fulfilling a perfectly instituted social order is the end of both history and of human evolution; the idea that a limitless historical actor (the liberal West—the privileged agent of history) could lead the way to such a perfectly instituted social order; and the metaphor of a developmental road stretching from particularism to universalism. In this context, Telleria observes how "one of the main contradictions of the human development reports is that the UNDP explicitly defends the notion that diversity is positive for human development; however, it implicitly assumes that the West—more specifically, its allegedly ideal and universal cultural values and principles—is the example that should guide the evolution of humankind."[98]

As well as imposing these approaches on others, this view of development locks participants into fixed models of progress: Rist stresses how the necessity of development becomes a shared belief across national leaders, international organizations, technocratic experts and the population at large, giving rise to "social constraints, expressed in the form of obligatory practices reinforcing commitment to the belief."[99] In this context, the rise of metrics and measurement plays a particularly significant role: the use of ordinal rankings among countries (on whatever measure) "unsettles national autonomy" and "places nations in a competitive and hierarchical space."[100] Thus, "Nations are locked in an increasing battery of measures to evaluate and rank them, like it or not. There is no prospect for a nation to opt out of this process by claiming it is operating with principles that are incommensurable with such metrics—which will be applied, come what may."[101]

These criticisms apply of course to development in general, rather than to social cohesion in particular. But it is nevertheless striking how smoothly social cohesion slides into these approaches. It either becomes added to a preexisting shopping list of 'good things' that form part of development strategies, or it becomes a kind of master organizing concept such that any measure relating to the social becomes justified in the name of 'social cohesion,' allowing even contradictory policies to be framed and justified in terms of reducing fragmentation, exclusion, and instability. Moreover, linking social cohesion to an idea of development hastens its transformation into a benchmark for measuring progress—whether as an ideal one (that is unachievable but can be worked towards) or as an 'attainable objective.' This then reinforces a sense that it is an uncomplicated good and—therefore—that we cannot have too much of it. When combined with a universalist model of social cohesion—often rooted essentially in Western understandings of what social cohesion is—this presents an uncontestable path for nations to follow. Here the more 'idealistic' versions of social cohesion may be even more constraining—at least recognizing it as an achievable goal suggests we might get there and decide whether or not we like it. An ideal endlessly defers this, locking us into a path whose end we never reach. In the international context, where agencies appear in some sense as 'outsiders' imposing their plans on existing nations, it is easy to see how this approach can be used in a disciplinary manner: 'we'll be back in two years to see how you've been getting on; and we expect to see results.'

This sense of imposing models from the outside is a recurring issue in these documents. It is of course starkest in the OECD's insistence on tying development to a particular set of economic reforms, which puts into question their commitments to broader, capacity-based models of development.[102] But it appears no less clearly in the various UN agencies' regional interventions. We have already noted how Arab leaders invoked the history of imperialism to question the idea of an externally imposed social cohesion, but the document on Myanmar gives an even more striking example: it highlights the importance of "a bottom up, iterative and consultative process, with stakeholders (experts, academics, CSOs, NSAs and government officials) from all ethnic states" in order to ensure "a locally owned and relevant framework for fostering social cohesion in Myanmar."[103] It admits, however, that "numerous stakeholders have struggled to identify a term that adequately explains the complexity and multi-dimensionality of the force, or 'glue,' that holds a society together and enables its members to peacefully coexist and develop."[104] The document even maintains that in Myanmar, "a country of great ethnic and religious diversity, there is no commonly accepted understanding or concept of social cohesion . . . either across the diverse array of languages, or within the dominant language of Myanmar itself."[105] Furthermore, "Multiple definitions of social cohesion were suggested during consultations with diverse stakeholders. A number of definitions refer to 'unity'—with somewhat negative connotations and seen as a coming together of peoples by a degree of force. Other definitions were said to be missing a key component, which was later defined as akin to 'peace,' 'coexistence,' 'tolerance' or 'living harmoniously' with their neighbours."[106]

The implication here is that social cohesion already has a clear meaning which is hard to get across or render in a particular (in this case local) language. Thus, the desire to give ownership to local stakeholders in Myanmar runs up against the problem that they might understand the concept in a radically different way (or indeed not at all). A similar tension can be observed in the UNDP's 2020 report, which emphasizes how "social cohesion may well be a contested concept within countries and contexts, subject to a wide variety of interpretations that may or may not conform to UN human rights values in spirit."[107] Its response to this, however, is to stress the necessity to "de-politicize the social cohesion agenda, so it becomes an agenda for peacebuilding and development consensus"[108] and later to stress that "sustainable social cohesion means advancing the values of UN norms on fundamental human rights: dignity of the person, human security, and opportunities for individual and collective development."[109]

There is no reason to believe that these commitments do not represent a sincere desire to respect local and regional differences, achieve democratic legitimacy through consultation and participation, and avoid imposing a one size fits all solution.[110] At the same time, it persistently runs up against the drive towards universalism. In particular, at no point does the Myanmar document raise the question of whether *anyone* really knows what social cohesion means—the lack of a referent in local languages is presented as a problem of applying and adopting the concept, but is not allowed to unsettle the concept itself.[111] This is perhaps particularly striking because the more 'negative' definition invoked by some in Myanmar clearly is part of the history of the concept (as illustrated by the example from Bertrand Russell in chapter 1). By now, however, the 'thickened' universalist approach is so ingrained that it cannot be called into question, but only 'modified.'

In this context, the call to 'depoliticize' social cohesion is particularly striking. While the authors of this sentence no doubt want to avoid the social cohesion agenda being linked to some particular political party or becoming a 'political football,' depoliticization is precisely part of the problem. Treating social cohesion as something with a settled meaning that is beyond politics and in the realm of objective measurement and benchmarked goals makes it harder to criticize policies enacted in its name. Rather than depoliticize the concept, we suggest it would be better to *repoliticize* it—to bring its contested character into view not as a qualifier or caveat before proceeding with the serious work of clarifying it, but as part of serious democratic deliberation within political and social institutions. In this respect, it is worth noting that the most recent document provided by the UN's Economic Commission for Latin America and the Caribbean document adopts a slightly different approach, explicitly recognizing itself as acting in the light of an "explicitly democratic and equality-oriented focus."[112] Its approach is not to assume a prior meaning of social cohesion, but to articulate it through values about which it is very clear, and through concrete policy proposals that follow from them (including, for example, a minimum basic income). Those values and policies are contested, but when posed like this they are also *contestable* in a way that opens up political debate rather than closing it down. As we will argue in our final chapter, *if* it is worth continuing to talk about social cohesion at all, it will be necessary to do so in ways that permit and deepen this contestation.

4.4 CONCLUSION

In this chapter we looked at how the notion of social cohesion has been exported into the global arena through its use in international development policies. Just as in the European context, the policy discourse of the OECD and UN combines demands for measurement and clarity with a multiplication of definitions, as well as the tendency to elevate social cohesion to an ideal or goal, increasingly linked to other values and concepts. The context of international development further solidifies this elevation by linking the concept even more strongly to notions of development and progress. As social cohesion dovetails into development strategies—as either one goal among many or an organizing concept for all social policy—its veneer of scientific and normative legitimacy only thickens, further limiting space for criticism and contestation.

At the same time, the international development context adds an additional dimension to the extent that these programs often appear as outside impositions on developing nations based on a narrow conception of progress. When social cohesion becomes incorporated into these programs, it reproduces the risk of applying a culturally specific understanding of the social to diverse societies. In that context, we have seen a striking tension between a sincere desire to adapt social cohesion agendas to local conditions and secure legitimacy among local stakeholders and a desire to provide clear and comparable measures that allow for meaningful comparison and a push for a 'depoliticized' concept that can be neutrally applied. In contrast, we have suggested, the drive for depoliticization is part of the problem—it would be better, instead, to bring the political and contested character of social cohesion into full view. That is the task of our final chapter.

Chapter 5

Contesting Social Cohesion

Milton Friedman famously remarked, "Only a crisis—actual or perceived—produces real change. When that crisis occurs, the actions that are taken depend on the ideas that are lying around." Friedman saw his role, and that of the neoliberal thought collectives of which he was a part, as making sure that it was his ideas that were lying around, "to keep them alive and available until the politically impossible becomes the politically inevitable."[1] We are currently living through a crisis, or rather several different interconnected and interlocking crises; and as we hope we have demonstrated in the previous chapters, social cohesion is an idea that is very much lying around, and one that is being picked up and encouraged by various institutions. Our claim is that it would be better if the idea was not picked and remained on the ground; or, more precisely, that it should not be picked up unless and until it can be picked up *critically*.

5.1 ANATOMY OF A FUZZWORD

Our analysis suggests that approaching social cohesion critically is made significantly more difficult by the way it is actually used and articulated, and in several ways. The social cohesion discourse we have discussed largely *reflects* the political and economic contexts in which it emerges and is employed. Thus, its first appearance as an object of policy in the 1990s is as a response to perceived failures of the welfare state and the challenges of economic 'modernization.' There, social cohesion is closely associated with notions of human and social capital and is linked primarily to an active employment agenda: its immediate antonym is social exclusion, and so it comes to be understood primarily in terms of inclusion. It is thus located in a particular phase of the development of neoliberalism, connected especially to third-way politics. This is clearest in those accounts that stress social cohesion's being achieved through incorporation in the labor market, with the attendant critiques of inactive populations and 'passive solidarity' prominent in the early European Union and OECD discourse. More broadly, we might see the desire to both quantify and instrumentalize the social as at least consistent with what Wendy Brown calls neoliberalism's economization of everything,[2] or William Davies's description of it as "the *pursuit of the disenchantment of politics by economics*" (empasis in original).[3] In this context, we have suggested, it provides a *raison d'être* for state policy that does not depend on traditional ideologies of left or right and remains compatible with a commitment to state neutrality regarding conceptions of the good life.

This narrowly economic view of social cohesion, however, comes rapidly to be complemented by a more substantive understanding connected to both emergent values and a growing concomitant interest in the quality of social relationships beyond mere economic inclusion: namely, as Davies characterizes it, by neoliberalism's "(re)discovery of the 'social'—or at least relational—dimensions of human behavior and subjective experience."[4] Thus we see the OECD enthusiastically adopting a capabilities approach while attempting to square this with both the strict requirements of neoliberal fiscal reform and the UN's developing substantive and value-laden understandings of social cohesion. Parallel with this is a growing desire to distinguish social cohesion from social capital, while yet retaining social capital and similarly depoliticized conceptions of civil society as measures of social cohesion, which combines with the tendency to instrumentalize social cohesion to flatten complex forms of social participation by reducing them to mere means (chapter 2).

In this historical context, social cohesion becomes increasingly 'thickened': it is loaded with different value concepts and defined in increasingly universalist—and normative—terms. At the same time, however, it remains marked by a kind of ontological realism that treats it as a single thing or substance that is isolable, measurable, and quantifiable through objective scientific analysis. And that leads to its becoming masked behind a veneer of scientific authority, presented as either value-neutral or as based on values that are sufficiently uncontroversial to treat them *as if* they were value-neutral. This in turn creates an impression of consensus that allows quite different policies to be grouped together in the name of social cohesion, while at the same time conveniently shielding these policies from criticism. Thus, it comes not only to reflect the contexts in which it emerges, but also to help *stabilize* those contexts, all too easily sliding into what Bourdieu and Wacquant call 'NewLiberalSpeak,' full of concepts that "do nothing but express, in a truncated and unrecognizable form (including to those who are promoting it), the complex and contested realities of a particular historical society, tacitly constituted into the model and measure of all things."[5]

One aspect of this stabilization is achieved through *neutralizing* possible criticisms—not least through the sheer complexity of the definitions posited and their relationships to other social goods and phenomena. We have pointed several times to the role of 'normative overdetermination' in inflating the concept's value: if a critic queries the value of social cohesion, they can be diverted by pointing to its instrumental connection to other social goods. If they then question this instrumental relationship, they can be pointed back to the thought that no one can really question the desirability of society holding together. And the more a socially cohesive society is invoked as an ideal, the more dissent and disagreement come to appear quixotic, if not irrational. Thus, for example, those Arab leaders who are concerned with a history of forced cohesion through colonial projects can be told that what they are worried about is not 'cohesion' but 'unity.' Or to put the point more comically, the online *Social Cohesion Hub*, produced by the German Institute of Development and Sustainability, encourages users to "browse the various concepts and definitions that are currently in use in the field to find a concept/term suitable for your needs" and asks "have you developed your own definition and conceptualisation and would like to share it with others? Tell us about it."[6]

In a certain sense, of course, the idea that social cohesion might tend to stabilize the *status quo* is unsurprising. It is, after all, a concept related to 'holding together,' and one that is mobilized in response to threats. Thus, Gregersen argues that it inevitably tends to pathologize dissent in a way that is incompatible with liberal values.[7] This risk is certainly real: consider for example the *Gilets Jaunes* (chapter 2). There is a streak within these discourses that sees social conflict as necessarily a threat to cohesion and seeks to minimize it, which can easily lead to the adoption of disciplinary measures or the assumption that attitudes and values need to be aligned. However, our argument goes further than this, suggesting that social cohesion's transformation into a 'fuzzword' obscures exactly what it claims to illuminate; and that it numbs critical faculties just when they are needed most. This explains, for example, why Gregersen can assert that the concept is necessarily illiberal while Dragolov et al. can see it as reflecting values of tolerance and plurality (chapter 2), and the OECD can even invoke in this context Rawls's quintessentially liberal idea of the well-ordered society (chapter 4). Certainly, then, the discourse of social cohesion serves to delegitimize dissent; but it does so less by demanding loyalty to a specific set of institutions than by allowing 'social cohesion' to lend a cover of legitimacy to policies that, shorn of cover, would otherwise be contested. For example, had the European Union proposed a 'get the unemployable back to work' agenda or a 'stop giving handouts to the poor' agenda it might have been the target of more critical scrutiny. More broadly, we have repeatedly seen how the bare fact that states have an interest in social order and stability becomes intertwined with and obscures more substantive value claims and concepts.

Social cohesion discourse furthermore *takes for granted* certain aspects of the *status quo*. This is perhaps clearest in the methodological nationalism that characterizes the claim that social cohesion is a property or feature of 'whole societies.' The idea of society is almost universally assumed to be co-extensive with the idea of the nation, meaning that social cohesion stops at national borders. This is problematic enough when focusing on historical European nation states, insofar as it entirely ignores 'cohesion' across borders (except as understood as cohesion *between* states, for example within the EU) and raises the question of the status of migrants within those groups. It is even more complex when the concept of social cohesion becomes linked to projects of nation-building through international development.[8] As we discussed in chapter 4, this risks *both* taking for granted and imposing a particular model of development on other nations, *and* assuming that existing state formations appropriately represent the populations within their territory. But as Buiter asks, "Under what circumstances and how can the concept of *country ownership* be relevant to a country with a myriad heterogenous and often conflicting views and interests?"[9]

Lastly, and more speculatively, we suggest that social cohesion discourse tends to reflect and further the *interests* of dominant groups and institutions. This claim remains more speculative because the kind of documentary analysis that we have undertaken here cannot clearly establish the links between these interests and either the formation of policies or their implementation on the ground. To do that would require deeper analysis of the interactions and intentions of specific agents and institutions. Nonetheless, as we have stressed, we can see clearly how social cohesion provides a convenient wrapping paper for quite diverse political agendas; and it would hardly be a surprise if it were the most powerful ideas that won out. More specifically, we might point to the repeated linking of social cohesion to economic growth, efficiency, and competitiveness even among some of the more critical policy documents discussed in chapters 3 and 4.

But in arguing that social cohesion tends to reflect and stabilize the *status quo* in this way, are we not drawing on controversial claims about the role of ideology? Are we not assuming a functional or teleological account, such that these ideas *necessarily* emerge out of their contemporary context and that their ubiquity is a matter solely of their capacity to stabilize that context?[10] The weight of this argument certainly needs to be acknowledged. But it would require a great deal of work to substantiate it. To put it bluntly, we are not attempting to settle the question of the nature and functioning of ideology. Rather our task is very much that of the under-laborer, working with much more modest presuppositions. First, the words, concepts, and metaphors we use *matter*.[11] The way in which we construct, represent, and articulate reality in turn shapes how we think about it.[12] Second, there are established routines of thinking and ways of doing things which tend to reproduce themselves unless they are actively challenged and unsettled. Unsettling them requires *effort*, in the sense both of actively subjecting them to critical scrutiny and of stopping and disrupting these routines. These disruptions become much harder the more these ideas are treated as objective reflections of reality or as ontological givens. Third, it is hardly controversial to point out that there are powerful and entrenched interests operating in our societies, and that the path of least resistance is often to frame discourse in ways that do not directly challenge those interests. This is all the more likely to occur in the sphere of politics and policymaking, but social research too can become implicated insofar as it sees itself serving the ends of policy. To the extent that there is a sense of ideology here, then, it is an extremely broad one.[13] Nothing we say here should be taken to imply that social cohesion is unique, or even particularly unusual, in this respect. Indeed, if our general approach is right, it can as well be applied to many other concepts. To take one example: the concept of *resilience* has undergone a similar trajectory to that of social cohesion and is often discussed alongside it.[14] This concept too appears to be on its way to becoming a fuzzword all of its own and has been criticized precisely for the way it largely takes for granted existing social structures and threats.[15]

That a concept serves to stabilize the *status quo* and neutralize criticism would already be reason enough to criticize it: even if one believes that the *status quo* is worth defending and stabilizing, the transformation of social cohesion into a fuzzword makes it harder to engage with those claims directly and subject them to critical scrutiny. It is thus in some sense already in tension with a commitment to democratic deliberation and accountability. However, this is made all the more problematic by the fact that there are many aspects of the current global system that clearly demand criticism. Some of these are the very things that social cohesion policies claim to address: poverty, social exclusion, and inequality. Some are issues that the discourse skates over, such as exploitation and domination (to which we will return in the next section). Still others are issues where the discourse of social cohesion is fatally compromised—the most significant of which is the urgency of the climate crisis, where the links between social cohesion and economic growth, progress and development are completely out of kilter with the demands of the moment.

With all of this in mind, it is tempting to throw up our hands and demand that we stop talking about social cohesion altogether. But it is too late for that. Social cohesion programs are well-embedded and multiplying. Political actors—whether they be social movements, local, regional, and national governments, civil service or community groups and activists—will have little choice but to confront such programs and engage with them at least partially *on their own terms*. If they are to do so in ways that do not merely reproduce the failings we have pointed to, they will have to look for ways to engage critically with this language in order to push beyond it. To return to where we left off the previous chapter, if the trend of such programs is to depoliticize social cohesion, the response will have to be to *politicize* it by opening it up to critical scrutiny and democratic debate. In what remains, we consider some ways in which this might be done.

5.2 SPACES AND RESOURCES OF CONTESTATION

To begin to unpick this thought, let us briefly return to the notion of buzzwords and fuzzwords we introduced in chapter 3. We can distinguish between three different responses to such terms. The first is implied by Ben Fine's trenchant critique of social capital. Fine points to social capital's essentially chaotic and contested meaning in ways that parallel some of our criticisms of social cohesion and concludes that "social capital has a content and dynamic that severely constrain progressive developmental thinking. It must be more heavily contested, but through argued rejection, in terms of its own inner weaknesses as well as its strategic consequences."[16] Thus, for Fine, the strategy is one of rejection and abandonment. The second is suggested by Gilbert Rist's proposal that "to neutralize the damaging power of a buzzword amounts to producing a down-to-earth definition that plainly states what it is all about and what it actually promotes."[17] Bringing the concept back down to earth might proceed in two directions. First, by focusing on how the concept is used in practice, by looking at the real interests it serves and its practical consequences, to *demystify* the concept by exposing its historically specific roots and to look at what it actually *does* when it is used.

Second, it might involve *deflating* the concept by consciously removing it from its association with particular policy programs, goals, values, and the assumption that it is intrinsically good. This is the thrust of the more particularist approach we discussed in chapter 2, which approaches social cohesion largely through the narrow question of what holds society together, without assuming that whatever is said to instantiate cohesion must be a good thing. Both are worthy goals, and we hope that our various criticisms might contribute to these projects. Nonetheless, while such deflationary strategies might be appropriate for social researchers, they are less likely to be sufficient on the terrain of practical politics, where the discourse remains suffused with values to which social actors will have to respond.

The third approach can be helpfully found in Neera Chandhoke's account of civil society:

> There was a time when civil society was interesting, even riveting, for political theorists, simply because rival and often acrimonious interpretations, formulations, and theorisations jostled with each other to impart meaning to the concept. There was a time, in other words, when civil society was an 'essentially contested' concept. Today it has become a consensual concept, a 'hurrah word,' and a matter of tiresomely unanimous acclaim. In the process, civil society has been flattened out.[18]

Yet, Chandhoke maintains, "for all the hubris associated with civil society, it remains a valuable term," since "by asserting civil society, people demand that regimes recognise the competence of the political public to chart out a discourse on the content and the limits of what is politically desirable and democratically permissible."[19] Thus, she argues, "It is critical to go beyond the buzzword that 'civil society' has become if it is to regain the vitality that it once had as an essentially contested concept."[20]

The notion of essentially contested concept is one we too have invoked, notably in chapter 2. In W. B. Gallie's classical account, essentially contested concepts are not merely concepts that have confused or unclear definitions, but rather are "concepts the proper use of which inevitably involves endless disputes about their proper uses on the part of their users."[21] This is what it means for them to be *essentially* contested—they are not merely contingently contested in such a way that this contestation is in principle resolvable. Rather it is the ongoing contestation that itself sustains the concept. If social cohesion is such a concept, then we might say the central problem with the approaches we have criticized is that they refuse to understand it as essentially contested, and that an insistence on definition, specification, operationalizability, and comparison is misplaced.[22]

The first step, then, would be to insist on recognizing social cohesion *as* contested, and to resist the drive to see it as something specific, distinct, and independent of our different interpretations and articulations of its meaning. The next step, however, is to actively *contest* its meaning. As we pointed out in the introduction, the rise of the discourse of social cohesion has been accompanied by a more critical undercurrent, one pointing to some of the dangers discussed in later chapters. Consider as an example Bernard's 1999 argument that social cohesion is a quasi-concept, an argument frequently cited in defense of the notion. What is less frequently noted is his argument that "it would be very risky to turn our backs on this concept, which is not merely a cover for growing inequalities but can open vistas of important debates. Instead, we must grasp it ... critique it and push it to its fullest logical extent, show that it necessarily maintains strong links to the principles of equality and social justice."[23] Likewise, Maloutas and Malouta suggest that "Social cohesion and governance would become real stakes if radical discourse and politics [were to] try to invest them with content and meaning that effectively transgress their legitimating function of conservative social regulation, and create massive demand for more social justice both in terms of redistributive justice and of democracy."[24] Both accounts, then, suggest that it might be possible to infuse the idea of social cohesion with a more radical content in ways that push it beyond its current usage.[25]

Cornwall and Brock offer a slightly different approach to infusing social cohesion, one that draws on Ernesto Laclau's language of 'chains of equivalence': "strings of words that work together to evoke a particular set of meanings."[26] They observe how the ways in which different concepts become linked together in policy and development discourses allow certain elements to dominate and fix something's meaning. This, however, also makes it possible to push other concepts to the fore and unsettle these meanings. Thus, for example, in the context of the buzzword 'participation,' they note, "In configuration with words like social justice, redistribution and solidarity, there is little place for talk about participation involving users as consumers, nor about poor people being empowered through the marketisation of services that were once their basic right."[27] Similarly, if social cohesion's strong conceptual connection with inclusion and participation tends to depoliticize and reduce it to instrumental value, this might be displaced by bringing forward those concepts that demand a deeper criticism of the *status quo*.

There are thus two senses of contestation here: First, openly recognizing social cohesion as open to contestation by different actors within society, rather than presented as a single essence or substance with a universal and uncontroversial meaning. This means being as clear as possible about the values and agendas to which it is linked and the purposes it serves. Second, directly contesting the framings and discourses of social cohesion that tend to reinforce and stabilize the status quo by pushing forward those elements of it that allow for a deeper criticism of the present, maintaining their critical edge and refusing to allow it to be blunted or neutralized. How precisely this second sense of contestation proceeds will of course depend on the values and perspectives of those doing the contesting. For our part, however, we suggest it might best proceed by emphasizing those elements that go beyond the narrow, depoliticized notions of 'social participation' and 'inclusion' and allow the idea itself to be subjected to democratic contestation and debate by those whom it supposedly serves. In what remains of the book, then, we want to consider some elements of the social cohesion discourse where we see the most promising opportunities to pursue these lines of contestation. In doing so we necessarily move beyond the core, critical argument of the book and invoke values that might be more controversial and that we do not explicitly defend here. We hope that, even if readers prefer other values, these still serve as useful examples of how different political projects might respond to and shape this discourse.

5.2.1 (In)Equality

One place to look to in order to push social cohesion discourse in a more critical direction might be equality. Some sort of idea of equality has in fact been prominent in the discourse from its earliest roots. The EU's Eurofound research in the early 1990s, for instance, was framed in terms of 'bridging the gap' between poor and rich, and countering the development of inequality; but the proposed solution—an active employment policy—was more concerned with getting people into work than directly addressing inequality through redistribution. Nonetheless, over time inequality came increasingly into focus. Thus, the Social Cohesion Radar that we focused on in chapter 2 separates equality from social cohesion analytically but stresses that "gaping inequalities undermine cohesion" and that their findings "support the notion that equality leads to social well-being."[28] The approach stressed by the UN's Economic Commission for Latin America and the Caribbean (ECLAC) goes significantly further, viewing social cohesion directly through "an explicitly democratic and equality-oriented focus" and emphasizing equality as a specific goal of social cohesion programs.[29]

In that sense, the literature on social cohesion can be placed in the context of what Mike Savage has called the "return of inequality" in recent decades, especially following the financial crisis of 2008.[30] High profile interventions like those of Richard Wilkinson and Kate Pickett's *The Spirit Level* and Thomas Piketty's *Capital in the Twenty-First Century* put the problem of *inequality* back to the center of public discourse.[31] As Savage notes, a striking feature of this is an interest in inequality among elites of various kinds, symbolized by Barack Obama's claim that inequality was the "the defining challenge of our time,"[32] and the World Economic Forum's identification of inequality as an existential threat.[33] In fact, it is not only elites who have invoked inequality, as is vividly demonstrated by the popularity of the Occupy slogan "We are the 99%."

One important way that the question of inequality might be radicalized is through Savage's suggestion that we push beyond a focus on income inequality to wealth inequality. For while income inequality clearly does matter, it is dwarfed by the rise in wealth inequality. This is particularly significant, since wealth inequality does not clearly track income inequality. While the United States stands out as having high levels of both, countries that we might traditionally think of as more egalitarian (and which tend to be represented as more socially cohesive) such as Germany, Austria, and the Nordic countries have some of the highest inequalities of wealth.[34] Grasping inequality in terms of wealth might thus challenge the framing of the European core as a model of cohesion to be followed by others.

As Savage stresses, a focus on wealth also radicalizes the picture in another way, by opening the question of how that wealth was acquired and accumulated, and by linking it to specific forms of power in the present. This is because "capital represents the hold of the old over the young, the dead over the living, and the power of existing asset holders compared to those who rely on selling their labor power today."[35] Focusing on accumulated and transmitted wealth thus opens up discussion of how histories of extraction and exploitation continue to mark the present in a way that a snapshot of income distribution does not. In turn it also brings into clearer view what Savage calls "visceral inequality," in which "the stuff of inequality is increasingly rendered as visceral, physical, and embodied, rather than abstracted into relative categories."[36] In this way it helps make connections between forms of economic domination, extraction and exclusion and those categories that are sometimes artificially hived off into the category of 'identity' (race and gender, for example).

A further radicalizing opportunity again emerges through equality when we consider the difference between seeing *inequality* as a threat to social cohesion and valuing *equality* itself. It is primarily the fear of inequality's deleterious effects that motivates the drive to relate it to social cohesion. Framed like this, inequality is something to minimize: but that does not have to be combined with a more explicitly egalitarian politics. In contrast, foregrounding *equality* might well go beyond a merely redistributive economic policy to think about social and political practices that affirm a deeper sense of equality, intimately connected to ideas of democracy and our capacity to *count as* and *cooperate as* equals.[37] In this way, an idea of equality might in turn radicalize the notion of participation away from merely incorporation into an existing (usually economically defined) social fabric, towards a more substantive vision of democratic social cooperation.

5.2.2 Solidarity

As with equality, the concept of solidarity is frequently invoked alongside that of social cohesion. Unlike equality, however, it is sometimes presented as if it were simply synonymous with social cohesion: as we have shown, it often forms part of both a scientific genealogy that goes back as least as far as Durkheim's analysis of organic and mechanical solidarity and of a political genealogy that traces it to certain aspects of the European ideal (most obviously the revolutionary demand for fraternity). However, there are important ways in which the concept of solidarity might be employed more critically. Crucially, as with the notion of civil society, it is frequently invoked by those who do not seek to stabilize or hold together existing society, but rather to challenge it. The socialist labor movement, for example, has historically seen the principle of solidarity in working-class life as providing a challenge to the stability of capitalist society while at the same time forming the basis of an alternative to it.[38] Anarchists have similarly seen practices of mutual aid not only as a way of surviving and 'helping out,' but as part of a "prefigurative" strategy for creating alternative societies.[39] An important element of this is an understanding of solidarity as recognition of shared interest and therefore a shared stake in a future in which those interests are realized or suppressed,[40] thus distinguishing solidarity from altruistic generosity or 'helping out,' encapsulated in the slogan 'solidarity not charity'—a distinction which is completely occluded when social cohesion is measured through people's willingness to help others or donate to charity.

Take, for example, the mutual aid groups that arose in response to COVID-19. Understood in terms of social cohesion, these can be seen as both reflective of high levels of social cohesion and as contributing to greater social cohesion. But, while mutual aid in this context clearly does 'help hold society together' and mitigate some extremes of deprivation and exclusion, activists using the term, 'mutual aid,' were—more or less self-consciously—drawing on a long tradition that sees mutual aid as a challenge to the existing order of things. Such activists have a vision of society that is based on radically different principles and the solidarity and co-operation underpinning their organizations is consciously counterposed to the competitive and hierarchical forms of cooperation that characterizes business as usual.[41] They thus grapple directly with the question of how to maintain a radical horizon and avoid simply plugging gaps in the existing structure. Approaching these activists in terms of social cohesion, however, at best grasps only one aspect of this dynamic—that society's continued existence depends on underlying forms of solidarity and co-operation—while completely ignoring the utopian possibilities it contains. Being reduced to a social cohesion strategy is precisely what these activists seek to avoid.[42] None of this is to insist that this is the only way that solidarity might be understood; but it is a tradition of thinking about solidarity to which social cohesion discourse is largely blind.

A second important ambivalence in 'solidarity' is that between seeing solidarity as a preexisting given and seeing it as something politically constructed in and between different groups. This is an extremely schematic distinction that simplifies many complex debates, but it is useful insofar as it raises the question of whether or not we ought to see solidarity as a kind of reflexive presocial set of attitudes towards those with which we share some common objective features or as something that is constructed out of practical cooperation in specific contexts. Of course, these are not mutually exclusive: one reading of the Marxist tradition is precisely in terms of helping people come to recognize their common interests *through* shared social and political struggles;[43] for Kropotkin, mutual aid is both a factor of evolution and something that must be exercised and practiced in order to strengthen and deepen it.[44] Nonetheless, the idea of solidarity as something to be built and performed is, crucially, something that the social cohesion discourse is unable fully to grasp. Instead, social cohesion tends to treat solidarity as a substance or a resource to be drawn on, lying 'out there,' a "human sociality beyond speech and history," as Rowan Williams puts it.[45]

Bringing solidarity to the fore also takes us back to the question of scope, largely in the background since chapter 1. The dominant approach to measuring and accounting for social cohesion sees it as a society-wide phenomenon, reifying, as we have argued, existing societies, usually within the boundaries of nation states. Invoking 'solidarity' already unsettles this insofar as it is possible to point to instances of cross-border solidarities within and among migrants who reject easy categorization in terms of a single state or society.[46] But this does not just miss the solidarities to be found at the edges of society; it also misses forms of solidarity that might emerge at a smaller scale among and between specific social groups. The point is not that these could not be aggregated at some overall social level—the point is that doing so misses important aspects of their specificity and reduces them into supports for, or challenges to, social cohesion, thus reinforcing the sense that social relations are primarily of *instrumental* value. Taking solidarity seriously as an object of study requires attending to the specific ways in which people build and practice solidarity; taking solidarity seriously as a political value requires exercising it.[47]

5.2.3 Pluralism

Various forms of pluralism, as we have seen, also play an important role in social cohesion discourse. As we discussed in chapter 1, these accounts often see social cohesion as necessarily responsive to value pluralism in modern societies, and in turn suggest that pluralism ought to be built into accounts of cohesion, at least through the values of tolerance of diversity and a resistance to demanding agreement on substantive values. In the previous chapters, we have been critical of these commitments because they tend to present values such as tolerance and diversity as somehow less controversial than other values: at worst, they risk producing and reproducing exclusions *in the name of* diversity, for example in linking diversity and pluralism to specific national and cultural identities, as we show in the course of discussing the inclusion of tolerance on the list of British values to be taught in schools in chapter 2. This is a particular risk in the context of international development, where ideas of diversity and pluralism sit alongside fairly narrow visions of legitimate development. Thus, for example, Telleria observes that "one of the main contradictions of the human development reports is that the UNDP explicitly defends the notion that diversity is positive for human development; however, it implicitly assumes that the West—more specifically, its allegedly ideal and universal cultural values and principles—is the example that should guide the evolution of humankind."[48]

However, as we stressed in chapter 4, these approaches often sit alongside a sincere desire for a more 'bottom-up' approach that recognizes specific cultural contexts and refuses a 'one size fits all' solution. What is important is that, in this context, the value of pluralism might be pushed forward and deepened in a way that challenges the very idea of a single, measurable and quantifiable notion of social cohesion and a narrow, circumscribed path of development towards it. Doing so would require challenging universalist framings in favor of greater attention to local practices and values. It might also involve stressing the incommensurability of certain values and ways of life. For example, Arturo Escobar, among others, has developed the idea of the 'pluriverse' expressed in the Zapatista desire for "a world in which many worlds might fit." For Escobar, "whereas the West has managed to universalize its own idea of the world, which only modern science can know and thoroughly study, the notion of the pluriverse inverts this seductive formula, suggesting pluriversality as a shared project based on a multiplicity of worlds and ways of worlding life."[49] The point of this is not simply to acknowledge that there are many different ways in which people can live together and thrive, but to mobilize this fact to challenge any framework that tends to homogenize and hegemonize the diversity of social life. In turn, it calls us to pay close attention to how values are articulated outside of development frameworks—for example through the concept of *Buen Vivir* (Good Living).[50] These are concepts that rest on the importance of complex relational goods that resist logics of quantification and maximization, and, like the previous example of solidarity, are less likely to surface if approached only at the scale of 'whole societies.'

Moreover, some elements of social cohesion discourse can clearly be mobilized *against* narrow and enforced national identities. In chapter 2, we noted Dragolov et al.'s observation that national belonging, while popularly considered to be necessary for social cohesion, represents something of an outlier, one not correlated with its other dimensions. Whether or not this tells us anything about 'social cohesion,' it clearly offers a basis for criticizing the common-sense idea that encouraging national identification and belonging is good for fostering social cooperation, trust and well-being. As well as directly challenging the idea that migration or multiculturalism are necessarily threats, it might be pushed even further against methodological nationalism itself;

rather than asking "is national identification good for social cohesion?" we might instead begin to ask deeper questions about how we understand society, its borders, and its limits. As with the issue of migrant solidarity, this opens up questions of cosmopolitanism, different forms of belonging, and how we define citizenship and membership in political communities.[51] Finally, a deeper commitment to pluralism might allow a more reflexive approach to the question of social conflict. Rather than assume either that conflict needs to be minimized or that it can be avoided merely through tolerance and acceptance, it might be possible to think of conflict—in the form of protests and contentious social movements, for example—as valuable for both revealing and addressing deeper social problems and generating new forms of social identity and belonging.

5.2.4 Common Good

The final area where we see scope for pushing social cohesion discourse beyond its current limits is that of the common good. The idea of an orientation on the common good was a central part of the Social Cohesion Radar that we discussed in chapter 2, introduced as a distinctive element understood as neither horizontal nor vertical but rather as one that "manifests itself in the level of solidarity and helpfulness, people's willingness to abide by social rules, and civic participation."[52] There is, though, an important ambiguity in what we mean when we talk about the common good. One way of thinking about the common good is simply as the aggregate of the individual goods of all members of society, so that pursuing a common good, in this framing, would be to pursue the outcomes that maximize this aggregate, and an orientation towards the common good would thus simply involve attention to the good of others. This is what seems to be implied when 'orientation on the common good' is measured by things like people helping out, volunteering, donating to charity, and so forth. However, as Alasdair MacIntyre insists, it is also possible to think about the common good of a group as something irreducible to the individual goods of each of its members, as something that "cannot be constructed out of what were the goods of its individual members, antecedently to and independently of their membership in it."[53] Such goods are "not only achieved by means of cooperative activity and shared understanding of their significance, but in key part constituted by cooperative activity and shared understanding of their significance."[54]

On this latter view, questions of the common good and questions of individual goods are neither identical nor clearly separable. Thus this is a distinctively *political* notion of the common good, insofar as it is articulated only through political deliberation and as part of a political community, one in which "individuals are always able to put in question through communal deliberation what has hitherto by custom and tradition been taken for granted both about their own good and the good of the community."[55] Here, we might note the significance of the sports team metaphor that has sometimes been employed to describe socially cohesive societies.[56] On the one hand, the good of a sports team is not reducible to the good of its members, for while it's true that members of a team help each other out, that is because they have the shared goal of winning. On the other hand, the goods of a sports team are clearly circumscribed, set by the rules of the game. There might be debate about *strategies*, even what counts as *success* in a given context, but the overall purposes and goals are predetermined. The good of societies and communities, however, is not like this—rather it is something *manifested in* and *grasped through* contestation and debate. Following MacIntyre, "Our primary shared and common good is found in that activity of communal learning through which we together become able to order goods, both in our individual lives and in the political society."[57]

While at times this latter conception of the common good does seem to be invoked in social cohesion discourse, it is often limited by the extremely thin conceptions of participation and co-operation that we have already criticized. These approaches tend to depoliticize and flatten forms of participation, ignoring their specific ideological and political context. Thus, civic participation is reduced to various formal mechanisms of engagement with politics. This, then opens up a further dimension of the critique developed in chapter 2, in terms of tending to conflate these two senses of the common good in a way that reduces the latter to the former. That is to say, the idea of a common good is invoked in a way that suggests the importance of shared goals, meanings, and social cooperation, while in practice its significance is reduced to merely volunteering and donating to charity. This is particularly important, since it is a frequent criticism of neoliberalism that it not only fails to grasp the importance of the common good in the latter sense, but that it systematically undermines the institutions and contexts in which such common goods can be debated, articulated, and realized. For Dardot and Laval, for example, under neoliberalism, "Citizenship is no longer defined as active participation in the definition of a common good specific to a political community, but as a permanent mobilization of individuals who must engage in partnerships and contracts of all kinds with enterprises and associations for producing local goods that provide consumers with satisfaction."[58]

At the same time, precisely because these accounts conflate these two senses of 'common good,' they also provide resources for pushing back. Rather than accepting the thin conception of common good, it is possible—and necessary—openly to contest its meaning. This, in turn, opens up questions of the practical contexts, spaces, and institutions that might permit greater democratic deliberation, whether they be the democratic repertoires of new social movements,[59] experiments in direct and participatory democracy,[60] drives to renew and enhance local and municipal government,[61] or questions of public ownership and the commons.[62]

5.3 CONCLUSION

In this final chapter, we have tried to bring together our criticisms of the dominant ways that the concept of social cohesion is used in social policy and international development and in the policy and social research that serves it. We have argued that the dominant framings make it harder to approach social cohesion critically as they tend to reflect and stabilize the contexts in which they emerge. Despite being presented in the name of reform or responding to urgent crises, these framings take very largely for granted elements of the *status quo* that shield them from deeper criticism. This is compounded by the way that social cohesion is frequently presented as an incontestable or uncontroversial good. These criticisms give good reason to be cautious about using the term social cohesion *at all*, but given that the term does not seem likely to disappear from use any time soon, we have argued that its meaning at least needs to be opened up to contestation. We have therefore suggested four concepts with which social cohesion is often associated as a possible grounding for such contestation as a means of rescuing what can be rescued from a discourse that might otherwise be better abandoned. These concepts—equality, solidarity, pluralism, and the common good—all encompass possibilities for pushing the discourse beyond its current limits by starting with elements already present within it. We are under no illusion that these are the only such concepts—for example, a similar critical procedure might be performed with 'trust' or 'conflict.' Nor should any of these concepts be seen as a magic key or silver bullet—each is just as capable of being subsumed into a less critical agenda or becoming a buzzword of its own. In order to be pushed forward in this way—and here we are of course revealing our own value commitments—they will have to be linked clearly and directly to a commitment to meaningful democratic deliberation and control and to the creation and revitalization of the social spaces and institutions that might make it possible.

In closing, then, let us return to the question of who the book is for. Most of our criticism has been directed at international and supranational institutions, while in this chapter we have pointed to social movement activists developing forms of solidarity and democratic participation outside of state structures, while also indicating projects that can be encouraged and developed at different levels of the state. Who, then, is to do the contesting? We see no particular reason to have to choose—just as social cohesion discourse pops up at many different levels, so do opportunities for contestation. This does not, however, mean all spaces are equal. In particular, much of what we have criticized derives partially from the demands of policymakers for clear and calculable metrics, easily packaged programs, and catchy, communicable buzzwords. Thus, contesting social cohesion at the level of states and policymaking bodies will require deeper thought about how they can be reconfigured and transformed in a way that allows them more clearly to see and to feel the importance of the social, especially after decades of neoliberalism.[63] And, to return once more to the question of scope, it should also lead us to question whether existing nation states best serve this end. In the spirit of our democratic commitments, these are questions for everyone.

Notes

INTRODUCTION

1. IPSOS, *Social Cohesion in the Pandemic Age: A Global Perspective* (2020), 3, https://www.ipsos.com/sites/default/files/ct/news/documents/2020-10/report-social-cohesion-and-pandemic-2020.pdf.

2. British Academy, *The COVID Decade: Understanding the Long-term Societal Impacts of COVID-19* (London: The British Academy, 2021), 74. See also Fanny Lalot, Dominic Abrams, Jo Bradwood, Kaya Davies Hayon, and Isobel Platts-Dunn, "The Social Cohesion Investment: Communities That Invested in Integration Programmes Are Showing Greater Social Cohesion in the Midst of the COVID-19 Pandemic," *Journal of Community & Applied Social Psychology* 32, no. 3 (2022): 536–54. https://doi.org/10.1002/casp.2522.

3. World Economic Forum, *The Global Risks Report 2022: 17th Edition* (Geneva: World Economic Forum, 2022).

4. For example, the WEF cites a poll describing "division in the country" as the number one concern of Americans as evidence of concerns over "social cohesion erosion"—thus fears of 'division' become articulated as worries about 'cohesion,' which can then in turn be plugged into a wider discourse (World Economic Forum, *The Global Risks Report 2022*, 17).

5. Paul Bernard, *Social Cohesion: A Critique*, Discussion Paper No. F/09 (Ottawa: Canadian Policy Research Networks, 1999); Thomas Maloutas and Maro Pantelidou Malouta, "The Glass Menagerie of Urban Governance and Social Cohesion: Concepts and Stakes / Concepts as Stakes," *International Journal of Urban and Regional Research* 28, no. 2 (2004): 449–65; Kasper J. Gregersen, "Assessing the Glue That Holds Society Together: Social Cohesion Arguments in Liberal Democracy," *Tidsskrift for Medier, Erkendelse Og Formidling* 1, no. 2 (2013): 78–94; Jan Dobbernack, *The Politics of Social Cohesion in Germany, France and the United Kingdom* (Basingstoke: Palgrave Macmillan, 2014).

6. Wendy Brown, *Undoing the Demos: Neoliberalism's Stealth Revolution* (New York: Zone Books, 2015); William Davies, *The Limits of Neoliberalism: Authority, Sovereignty and the Logic of Competition* (London: Sage Publications, 2014), 4.

CHAPTER 1

1. Bertrand Russell, *Reith Lectures 1948: Authority and the Individual*, "Lecture 1: Social Cohesion and Human Nature," 1948, 1, http://downloads.bbc.co.uk/rmhttp/radio4/transcripts/1948_reith1.pdf, accessed December 4, 2022.
2. Russell, *Reith Lectures*, 1.
3. Russell, *Reith Lectures*, 3.
4. Russell, *Reith Lectures*, 3.
5. Russell, *Reith Lectures*, 3.
6. Russell, *Reith Lectures*, 3.
7. Russell, *Reith Lectures*, 4.
8. Anna Rita Manca, "Social Cohesion," in *Encyclopedia of Quality of Life and Well-Being Research*, ed. Alex C. Michalos (Dordrecht: Springer, 2014), 6026. https://doi.org/10.1007/978-94-007-0753-5_2739.
9. We use the language of 'thick' and 'thin' somewhat broadly to denote how the concept begins to take on additional layers of meaning and significance beyond a narrow focus on 'holding together,' and especially as it begins to acquire normative significance and incorporate specific value concepts—in that sense we are drawing on the metaethical use of the term 'thick concept' to describe concepts that combine normative and descriptive content. This should not be confused with the way the distinction between thick and thin is sometimes applied to the difference between qualitative and quantitative research in the social sciences.
10. See Bujar Aruqaj, *Social Cohesion in European Societies: Conceptualising and Assessing Togetherness* (London and New York: Routledge, 2023), 23–25; Louis Moustakas, "A Bibliometric Analysis of Research on Social Cohesion from 1994–2020," *Publications* 10, no. 1 (2022). https:/doi.org/10.3390/publications10010005.
11. Georgi Dragolov, Zsófia S. Ignácz, Jan Lorenz, Jan Delhey, Klaus Boehnke, and Kai Unzicker, *Social Cohesion in the Western World: What Holds Societies Together: Insights from the Social Cohesion Radar* (Dordrecht: Springer, 2016), 2.
12. See, for example, Xavier Fonseca, Stephan Lukosch, and Frances Brazier, "Social Cohesion Revisited: A New Definition and How to Characterise It," *Innovation: The European Journal of Social Science Research* 32, no. 2 (2018): 231–53; Menno Fenger, "Deconstructing Social Cohesion: Towards an Analytical Frame for Assessing Social Cohesion Policies," *Corvinus Journal of Sociology and Social Policy* 3, no. 2 (2012): 39–54; Gianmaria Bottoni, "A Multilevel Measurement Model of Social Cohesion," *Social Indicators Research* 136, no. 3 (2018): 835–57.
13. Aruqaj notably offers a more detailed engagement with Durkheim's work than much of the literature, identifying social cohesion not with either mechanical or organic solidarity, but with his concept of collective consciousness, "which should be considered as the academic origin of social cohesion" (Aruqaj, *Social Cohesion*, 27). While more sophisticated, this still begs the question of why we should identify these two terms.
14. See Jan Dobbernack, *The Politics of Social Cohesion in Germany, France and the United Kingdom* (Basingstoke: Palgrave Macmillan, 2014), 24. Indeed, Durkheim's main intent, in the context of the Dreyfus Affair and panics over the

durability of the French Republican ideal, is to argue that modern society is less prone to disintegration and dissolution, and to analyze the ways that it holds together in spite of popular prejudices to the contrary. His starting point is thus very different from contemporary discourse that sees cohesion as in decline and in need of restoration, and to the extent that his analysis has policy consequences it involves celebrating the functional differentiation of different parts of society rather than encouraging a specific form of solidarity or shared identity.

15. Dragolov et al., *Social Cohesion in the Western World*, xxv.

16. See Dobbernack, *The Politics of Social Cohesion*, 23.

17. Gregersen refers to this as the "threat premise." J. Kasper Gregersen, "Assessing the Glue That Holds Society Together: Social Cohesion Arguments in Liberal Democracy," *Tidsskrift for Medier, Erkendelse Og Formidling* 1, no. 2 (2013): 78–94.

18. Chapter 3 provides examples of this at the European level. For discussion of it at the national level see Dobbernack, *The Politics of Social Cohesion*, chap. 3–5; Nils Holtug, *The Politics of Social Cohesion: Immigration, Community, and Justice* (Oxford: Oxford University Press, 2021), chap. 2; On sociological narratives of decline see Ray E. Pahl, "The Search for Social Cohesion: From Durkheim to the European Commission," *European Journal of Sociology* 32, no. 2 (1991): 345–60. DOI:10.1017/S0003975600006305.

19. Dobbernack, *The Politics of Social Cohesion*, 49–50.

20. Jane Jenson, *Mapping Social Cohesion: The State of Canadian Research*, Study No. F/03 (Ottawa: Canadian Policy Research Networks, 1998), 37.

21. Dobbernack, *The Politics of Social Cohesion*, 168.

22. OECD, *Societal Cohesion and the Globalising Economy: What Does the Future Hold?* (Paris: OECD, 1997), 7–8.

23. Dobbernack, *The Politics of Social Cohesion*, 66.

24. Gregersen, "Assessing the Glue," 82.

25. We are grateful to Matteo Gianni for pointing out that the critique of such approaches to social cohesion may be conceived as an anti-positivist endeavor, since the ontological realism assumption and the urge to detect and measure social cohesion obviously implies positivist epistemology. However, it is not our aim to develop a non-positivist alternative to the mainstream accounts of social cohesion in social science and policy discourse, since we are skeptical of the notion of social cohesion as such.

26. Eurofound, *Social Cohesion and Well-being in Europe* (Luxembourg: Publications Office of the European Union, 2018), 49.

27. Jacqueline Broadhead, *Social Cohesion in Europe: Literature Review* (The British Council, 2022), 5. https://www.britishcouncil.org/research-policy-insight/research-reports/social-cohesion.

28. Kim Sung-Geun, "Measuring Regional Social Cohesion by Objective Indices: The Case of Korea," *International Journal of Community Well-Being* 5, no. 3 (2022): 602.

29. The classical treatment is Wittgenstein's account of games in Ludwig Wittgenstein, *Philosophical Investigations*, trans. G. E. M. Anscombe (Oxford: Blackwell, 1967), 31–32. See also Bob Brecher, *Torture and the Ticking Time Bomb*

(Oxford: Blackwell, 2007), 3–6, for a discussion of the limits of demands for definition.

30. Friedrich Nietzsche, *On the Genealogy of Morals and Ecce Homo*, trans. Walter Kaufmann (New York: Vintage Books, 1989).

31. Likewise, the Canadian Government's Policy Research Sub-Committee on Social Cohesion defined it as "the ongoing process of developing a community of shared values, shared challenges and equal opportunity within Canada" (See Jenson, *Mapping Social Cohesion*).

32. Joseph Chan, Ho-Pong To, and Elaine Chan, "Reconsidering Social Cohesion: Developing a Definition and Analytical Framework for Empirical Research," *Social Indicators Research* 75 (2006): 281.

33. Dragolov et al., *Social Cohesion in the Western World*, 6.

34. Aruqaj, *Social Cohesion*, 27–34.

35. Aruqaj, *Social Cohesion*, 13.

36. In using this terminology we are following Jan Germen Janmaat, "Social Cohesion as a Real-life Phenomenon: Assessing the Explanatory Power of the Universalist and Particularist Perspectives," *Social Indicators Research* 100 (2011): 61–83.

37. We use the language of universalism and particularism to refer to the definition or characterization of social cohesion itself, but it is also sometimes used to distinguish between universal and particular *correlates* or *antecedents* of social cohesion. Thus, for example, the Social Cohesion Radar, which we discuss in detail in chapter 2, applies a universalist understanding of what social cohesion *is* to both Europe and Asia, in order to investigate whether its correlates are the same in both regions, distinguishing between "'universal' correlates of cohesion—country characteristics, which operate in the same manner in both world regions—and 'particularistic' correlates of cohesion, which work differently in the two world regions." See Jan Delhey, Klaus Boehnke, Georgi Dragolov, Zsófia Ignácz, Mandi Larsen, Jan Lorenz, and Michael Koch, "Social Cohesion and Its Correlates: A Comparison of Western and Asian Societies," *Comparative Sociology* 17, no. 3–4 (2018): 429.

38. Andy Green and Jan Germen Janmaat, *Regimes of Social Cohesion: Societies and the Crisis of Globalisation* (Basingstoke: Palgrave Macmillan, 2011), 18.

39. See Aruqaj, *Social Cohesion*, 41–45, for an impressive overview of these positions.

40. See Chan et al., "Reconsidering Social Cohesion," 293–98.

41. See, for example, Aruqaj, *Social Cohesion*, 41; Bottoni, "A Multilevel Measurement Model," 836; Chan et al., "Reconsidering Social Cohesion," 279.

42. See Green and Janmaat, *Regimes of Social Cohesion*, 3.

43. Dragolov et al., *Social Cohesion in the Western World*, viii.

44. Bottoni, "A Multilevel Measurement Model," 837.

45. Broadhead, *Social Cohesion in Europe*, 13.

46. Seongha Cho, "Economic Conditions and Social Cohesion: An Analysis of French European Social Survey Data," *French Politics* 20, no. 1 (2022): 26.

47. Dragolov et al., *Social Cohesion in the Western World*, 9.

48. Dragolov et al., *Social Cohesion in the Western World*, 11.

49. For example, Judith Maxwell, *Social Dimensions of Economic Growth* (Alberta: University of Alberta, 1996); EU, *Building the Knowledge Society: Social and Human Capital Interactions* (2003).

50. Holtug, *The Politics of Social Cohesion*, 74.

51. Holtug, *The Politics of Social Cohesion*, 74.

52. Holtug, *The Politics of Social Cohesion*, 74.

53. Holtug, *The Politics of Social Cohesion*, 74.

54. Dragolov et al., *Social Cohesion in the Western World*.

55. Aruqaj, *Social Cohesion*, 36.

56. Broadhead, *Social Cohesion in Europe*, 18.

57. Dragolov et al., *Social Cohesion in the Western World*, 6.

58. Maxwell, *Social Dimensions of Economic Growth*.

59. Policy Research Initiative, *Sustaining Growth, Human Development, and Social Cohesion in a Global World* (Government of Canada, 1999).

60. Ray Forrest and Ade Kearns, "Social Cohesion, Social Capital and the Neighbourhood," *Urban Studies* 38, no. 12 (2001): 2125–43.

61. Eurofound, *Social Cohesion and Well-Being in Europe*, 3.

62. Gregersen, "Assessing the Glue," 88.

63. Holtug, *The Politics of Social Cohesion*, 82.

64. For example, Dragolov et al., *Social Cohesion in the Western World*, chap. 2.

65. Regina Berger-Schmitt, *Social Cohesion as an Aspect of the Quality of Societies: Concept and Measurement* (Mannheim: Center for Survey Research and Methodology, 2000), 405.

66. Gregersen, "Assessing the Glue," 87.

67. However, again, the term 'social cohesion' only appears five times in Putnam's classic *Bowling Alone* and is not systematically developed as a concept. See Robert Putnam, *Bowling Alone* (New York: Simon & Schuster, 2000).

68. See Ben Fine, *Theories of Social Capital: Researchers Behaving Badly* (London: Pluto, 2010) for a critical account of the social capital's rise and promotion by the World Bank. See also Barbara Arneil, *Diverse Communities: The Problem with Social Capital* (Cambridge: Cambridge University Press, 2006).

69. See Putnam, *Bowling Alone*; Robert Putnam and Lewis M. Feldstein, *Better Together: Restoring the American Community* (New York: Simon & Schuster, 2004).

70. Aruqaj, *Social Cohesion*, 28. Though social cohesion is sometimes referred to as "a resource that supports people in difficult times" (Eileen E. Avery, Joan M. Hermsen, and Danielle C. Kuhl, "Toward a Better Understanding of Perceptions of Neighbourhood Social Cohesion in Rural and Urban Places," *Social Indicators Research* 157 [2021]: 536).

71. Dragolov et al., *Social Cohesion in the Western World*, 12.

72. Green and Janmaat, *Regimes of Social Cohesion*, 18–19.

73. Chan et al., "Reconsidering Social Cohesion," 291.

74. See also Aruqaj, *Social Cohesion*, 7.

75. Andreas Wimmer and Nina Glick Schiller, "Methodological Nationalism, the Social Sciences, and the Study of Migration: An Essay in Historical Epistemology," *International Migration Review* 37, no. 3 (2003): 577–78.

76. Wimmer and Glick Schiller, "Methodological Nationalism," 579.
77. Wimmer and Glick Schiller, "Methodological Nationalism," 578.
78. Policy Research Initiative, *Sustaining Growth.*
79. Forrest and Kearns, "Social Cohesion."
80. Manca, "Social Cohesion," 6026. Chan et al., "Reconsidering Social Cohesion," 290.
81. Dragolov et al., *Social Cohesion in the Western World,* 67.
82. Wimmer and Glick Schiller, "Methodological Nationalism," 579.
83. See, for example, Fenger, "Deconstructing Social Cohesion." Forrest and Kearns, "Social Cohesion."

CHAPTER 2

1. Joseph Chan, Ho-Pong To, and Elaine Chan, "Reconsidering Social Cohesion: Developing a Definition and Analytical Framework for Empirical Research," *Social Indicators Research* 75 (2006): 298.
2. Chan et al., "Reconsidering Social Cohesion," 279.
3. Chan et al., "Reconsidering Social Cohesion," 274.
4. Chan et al., "Reconsidering Social Cohesion," 290.
5. Chan et al., "Reconsidering Social Cohesion," 280.
6. Chan et al., "Reconsidering Social Cohesion," 289.
7. Chan et al., "Reconsidering Social Cohesion," 291.
8. Chan et al., "Reconsidering Social Cohesion," 290.
9. This becomes conceptualized in terms of a two-by-two grid of horizontal-subjective (concerning attitudes towards other citizens), horizontal-objective (concerning behavior towards other citizens), vertical-subjective (concerning attitudes towards political and social institutions) and vertical-objective (concerning behavior towards political and social institutions). Even when Chan et al.'s approach is not adopted wholesale, this grid framing is regularly invoked in policy literature, especially in the international development context (see Chan et al., "Reconsidering Social Cohesion," and chapter 4 of this book).
10. When using the term Social Cohesion Radar, we are referring to the measurement instrument itself, first outlined in Georgi Dragolov, Zsófia Ignácz, Jan Lorenz, Jan Delhey, and Klaus Boehnke, *The Social Cohesion Radar: Measuring Common Ground: An International Comparison of Social Cohesion* (Gütersloh: Bertelsmann Stiftung, 2013), addressed more specifically to the context and concerns of German policymakers and later presented in a scholarly monograph as Georgi Dragolov, Zsófia S. Ignácz, Jan Lorenz, Jan Delhey, Klaus Boehnke, and Kai Unzicker, *Social Cohesion in the Western World: What Holds Societies Together: Insights from the Social Cohesion Radar* (Dordrecht: Springer, 2016). While we draw mostly on the latter publication, there is considerable overlap between them, and so we generally refer to the Radar as a whole in the text.
11. The Bertelsmann Stiftung is a private philanthropic organization whose mission statement is "Inspiring people. Shaping the future. Participating in a globalized

world." Its project on social cohesion seeks to "measure social cohesion, thus providing a better understanding of current societal trends . . . [and] help communities activate their potential in strengthening cohesion and foster partnerships that improve communal life," https://www.bertelsmann-stiftung.de/en/our-projects/social-cohesion, accessed June 24, 2023.

12. Eurofound currently defines its "priorities for 2021–2024 [as] shaped by the key challenges for social cohesion and just transitions in a changing environment in the aftermath of the COVID-19 crisis," https://www.eurofound.europa.eu/about-eurofound/what-we-do, accessed June 24, 2023.

13. See Bertelsmann Stiftung, *What Holds Asian Societies Together? Insights from the Social Cohesion Radar* (Verlag Bertelsmann Stiftung, 2018); and Jan Delhey, Klaus Boehnke, Georgi Dragolov, Zsófia Ignácz, Mandi Larsen, Jan Lorenz, and Michael Koch, "Social Cohesion and Its Correlates: A Comparison of Western and Asian Societies," *Comparative Sociology* 17, no. 3–4 (2018): 426–55. Applying the concept to Asian societies necessarily required using some different survey data and adapting indicators to local context, but the core conceptualization of 'social cohesion' and its set of domains and dimensions was retained.

14. Paul Bernard, *Social Cohesion: A Critique*, Discussion Paper No. F/09 (Ottawa: Canadian Policy Research Networks, 1999), 24.

15. Georgi Dragolov, Zsófia S. Ignácz, Jan Lorenz, Jan Delhey, Klaus Boehnke, and Kai Unzicker, *Social Cohesion in the Western World: What Holds Societies Together: Insights from the Social Cohesion Radar* (Dordrecht: Springer, 2016), viii.

16. Dragolov et al., *Social Cohesion in the Western World*, 6.

17. Dragolov et al., *Social Cohesion in the Western World*, 7, Table 1.1.

18. Dragolov et al., *Social Cohesion in the Western World*, 25.

19. Dragolov et al., *Social Cohesion in the Western World*, vi.

20. Aruqaj notes how aggregation at the national level can also paper over deep divisions among regions and groups, for example leading to the United States being represented as a highly cohesive society when attention to specific groups might paint a different picture (see Bujar Aruqaj, *Social Cohesion in European Societies: Conceptualising and Assessing Togetherness* [London and New York: Routledge, 2023], 90).

21. Chan et al., "Reconsidering Social Cohesion," 284.

22. Chan et al., "Reconsidering Social Cohesion," 288. Here they are directly challenging Berger-Schmitt (2000) who includes 'equality of opportunity' as a component of social cohesion.

23. In this respect, they are following Schieffer and van der Noll, who argue that there is stronger consensus in the literature than sometimes suggested. David Schiefer and Jolanda van der Noll, "The Essentials of Social Cohesion: A Literature Review,'" *Social Indicators Research* 132 (2017): 579–603.

24. Dragolov et al., *Social Cohesion in the Western World*, xxviii.

25. Dragolov et al., *Social Cohesion in the Western World*, 15.

26. Dragolov et al., *Social Cohesion in the Western World*, 11.

27. Dragolov et al., *Social Cohesion in the Western World*, 111.

28. Dragolov et al., *Social Cohesion in the Western World*, 11.

29. Less prominently, another value concept appears to sneak in when among the indicators of "perception of fairness" is included people's level of agreement with the claim that "government should reduce differences in income levels" (Dragolov et al., *Social Cohesion in the Western World*, 27, Table 2.3). While other indicators of this dimension concern concepts that, while normatively loaded and subject to multiple interpretations, are generally agreed to be positive or negative (fairness and corruption), this suggests a commitment to egalitarianism that is more controversial and substantive.

30. Dragolov et al., *Social Cohesion in the Western World*, 23.

31. Dragolov et al., *Social Cohesion in the Western World*, 11. Thus, Aruqaj criticizes the characterization of this as a value-judgment, arguing that "acceptance of diversity or openness can also be seen as having a purely functional importance to societal cohesion" in modern societies (Aruqaj, *Social Cohesion*, 51).

32. Chan et al., "Reconsidering Social Cohesion," 292.

33. Dragolov et al., *Social Cohesion in the Western World*, 80.

34. Dragolov et al., *Social Cohesion in the Western World*, 81, Table 6.1.

35. Dragolov et al., *Social Cohesion in the Western World*, 83.

36. John Rawls, *Political Liberalism* (New York: Columbia University Press, 1995), 13.

37. Dragolov et al., *Social Cohesion in the Western World*, 43.

38. Dragolov et al., *Social Cohesion in the Western World*, 50. This identification of Durkheim's organic solidarity with equality and social justice is itself something of a stretch, since the central feature of organic solidarity is functional interdependence, which does not preclude either inequality or injustice.

39. Though, rather cryptically, they also suggest that this might be read as "strongly suggesting that there is a need to identify indicators that underlie an organic mode of identification with the geopolitical entity (here: the nation) in future measurement" (Dragolov et al., *Social Cohesion in the Western World*, 50), raising the question of how they know that the measures of pride and attachment they use do not already do this.

40. See Anna Lockley-Scott, "Towards a Critique of Fundamental British Values: The Case of the Classroom," *Journal of Beliefs & Values* 40, no. 3 (2019): 354–67; Ümit Yıldız, "An Anti-Racist Reading of the Notion of 'Fundamental British Values,'" *Prism* 3, no. 2 (2021): 91–107. More broadly, the concept of tolerance has historically been subject to various criticisms of its ideological and potentially conservative implications, for example, Robert Paul Wolff, Barrington Moore Jr., and Herbert Marcuse, *A Critique of Pure Tolerance* (London: Cape Editions, 1969).

41. See also Thomas Maloutas and Maro Pantelidou Malouta, "The Glass Menagerie of Urban Governance and Social Cohesion: Concepts and Stakes/ Concepts as Stakes," *International Journal of Urban and Regional Research* 28, no. 2 (2004): 458–62, for a critique of the connections between tolerance and social cohesion.

42. Chan et al., "Reconsidering Social Cohesion," 293.

43. Dragolov et al., *Social Cohesion in the Western World*, 21.

44. Dragolov et al., *Social Cohesion in the Western World*, 12.

45. The examples in this paragraph refer only to their findings from Western countries. The analysis of Asian countries found evidence for different correlates, leading them to warn policymakers about assuming they can easily apply the same policies across regions. Even in this comparison, however, "economic prosperity" is emphasized as a "universal" correlate. Jan Delhey, Klaus Boehnke, Georgi Dragolov, Zsófia Ignácz, Mandi Larsen, Jan Lorenz, and Michael Koch, "Social Cohesion and Its Correlates: A Comparison of Western and Asian Societies," *Comparative Sociology* 17, no. 3–4 (2018).

46. Dragolov et al., *Social Cohesion in the Western World*, 61.
47. Dragolov et al., *Social Cohesion in the Western World*, 64.
48. Dragolov et al., *Social Cohesion in the Western World*, 61.
49. Dragolov et al., *Social Cohesion in the Western World*, 64.
50. Dragolov et al., *Social Cohesion in the Western World*, xxx.
51. Dragolov et al., *Social Cohesion in the Western World*, 85.
52. Dragolov et al., *Social Cohesion in the Western World*, 65.
53. Eurofound, *Social Cohesion and Well-being in Europe*, 49.
54. Eurofound, *Social Cohesion and Well-being in Europe*, 1.

55. Chan et al. might respond to this by arguing that they are attempting to trace willingness to cooperate across social cleavages, and that these questions simply track the most significant contemporary social cleavages in the societies under investigation. This would be to accept that social cohesion *itself* does not depend on social and cultural context, but that its *measurement* requires knowledge of social and cultural context. This brings a risk of circularity, insofar as it assumes we already know what the major cleavages are when we set out to investigate them.

56. Chan et al., "Reconsidering Social Cohesion," 294–97.

57. Chan et al. do acknowledge that "depending on the specific context and political culture, what constitutes 'political participation' may have some variation across societies" (Chan et al., "Reconsidering Social Cohesion," 297), but what is at stake here is not the assumption that political participation is invariate but that it always uncomplicatedly contributes to cohesion in a comparable and aggregative manner.

58. Seongha Cho, "Economic Conditions and Social Cohesion: An Analysis of French European Social Survey Data," *French Politics* 20, no. 1 (2022): 26.

59. See, for example, Michael J. Carpenter and Benjamin Perrier, "Yellow Vests: Anti-austerity, Pro-democracy, and Popular (Not Populist)," *Frontiers in Political Science* 5 (2023): 1037942. doi: 10.3389/fpos.2023.1037942.

60. This might also suggest (along with the Social Cohesion Radar's emphasis on meeting friends and family in the 'connectedness' dimension) a greater dependence than is acknowledged on theories of social capital. While both approaches distinguish social cohesion from social capital based on their scope (see chapter 1), when it comes to measurement, the emphasis on voluntary associations and electoral participation closely maps the concerns of social capital theorists, opening it to similar criticisms of being insensitive to the qualitative dimension of these relationships, and thus in particular to relationships of power and exploitation. See Barbara Arneil, *Diverse Communities: The Problem with Social Capital* (Cambridge: Cambridge University

Press, 2006); Ben Fine, *Theories of Social Capital: Researchers Behaving Badly* (London: Pluto, 2010).

61. See Jean L. Cohen and Andrew Arato, *Civil Society and Political Theory* (Cambridge MA: The MIT Press, 1994); Neera Chandhoke, *State and Civil Society* (New Delhi: Sage Publications, 1995).

62. The existence and role of civil society in state socialist regimes was a central question for dissidents and analysts of Eastern Europe in the 1980s and 1990s.

63. See Cohen and Arato, *Civil Society and Political Theory*, part 1.

64. It might, of course, be suggested that civil society contributes to the cohesion of liberal democratic societies and undermines illiberal undemocratic ones. This, however, would be to accept either that "vibrancy of civil society" cannot always be a measure of social cohesion *or* to closely tie the concept of social cohesion to liberal democratic societies.

65. Dragolov et al., *The Social Cohesion Radar*, 51.

66. This parallels Arneil's critique of social capital: "If connectedness is simply a means *in order* to create other ends, the normative nature of these connections becomes largely irrelevant." Arneil, *Diverse Communities*, 225.

67. Dragolov et al., *Social Cohesion in the Western World*, xxv.

68. Andy Green and Jan Germen Janmaat, *Regimes of Social Cohesion: Societies and the Crisis of Globalisation* (Basingstoke: Palgrave Macmillan, 2011), 3.

69. Green and Janmaat, *Regimes of Social Cohesion*, 18.

70. Chan et al., "Reconsidering Social Cohesion," 290.

71. This, of course, rests on a distinction between coercion and consensus that might, when specified, reintroduce significant normative questions about, for example, the difference between active and passive consent or the relation between coercion, manipulation, and ideology.

72. Green and Janmaat, *Regimes of Social Cohesion*, 64.

73. Green and Janmaat, *Regimes of Social Cohesion*, 65.

74. Green and Janmaat, *Regimes of Social Cohesion*, 75.

75. Green and Janmaat, *Regimes of Social Cohesion*, 82.

76. See Green and Janmaat, *Regimes of Social Cohesion*, 94–96, Table 5.1.

77. Green and Janmaat, *Regimes of Social Cohesion*, 94.

78. Green and Janmaat, *Regimes of Social Cohesion*, 64.

79. See Gøsta Esping-Andersen, *The Three Worlds of Welfare Capitalism* (Cambridge: Polity Press, 1990), and criticism offered by Gregory J. Kasza, "The Illusion of Welfare 'Regimes,'" *Journal of Social Policy* 31, no. 2 (2002): 271–87.

80. Green and Janmaat, *Regimes of Social Cohesion*, 65.

81. Green and Janmaat, *Regimes of Social Cohesion*, 65.

82. Green and Janmaat, *Regimes of Social Cohesion*, 79–81.

83. Green and Janmaat, *Regimes of Social Cohesion*, 202–3.

84. Notably in this context, Green and Janmaat tend to identify the rise of neoliberalism as involving the return and renewal of the ideological tradition associated with the liberal regime (Green and Janmaat, *Regimes of Social Cohesion*, 49–50). While there are of course clear intellectual lineages between these traditions, doing so risks missing the specificity of neoliberalism, in particular the way it reconceptualizes

the state as no longer standing outside the market but participates in it as an equal player (and thus must subject itself to 'efficiencies' and 'cost-benefit analysis' like any business). See Pierre Dardot and Christian Laval, *The New Way of the World: On Neoliberal Society*, trans. Gregory Elliott (London: Verso, 2013), 301–2. Moreover, it also evades the question of how neoliberalism became hegemonic over other regimes and traditions, potentially ignoring elements from other traditions that also influenced neoliberalism's development (most obviously the Austrian school of Ordo-Liberalism).

85. In this context, we might even suggest that this approach is even more prone to methodological nationalism, insofar as it takes for granted a particular set of intellectual and political traditions that are directly connected to geographical units and national cultures.

86. Green and Janmaat, *Regimes of Social Cohesion*, 172.
87. Green and Janmaat, *Regimes of Social Cohesion*, 172.
88. Green and Janmaat, *Regimes of Social Cohesion*, 172.
89. Green and Janmaat, *Regimes of Social Cohesion*, 177.

CHAPTER 3

1. For example, Chan et al. (2006), discussed in the previous chapter, respond critically to Berger-Schmitt, whose concept is explicitly designed to reflect and respond to EU policy discourse. See Joseph Chan, Ho-Pong To, and Elaine Chan, "Reconsidering Social Cohesion: Developing a Definition and Analytical Framework for Empirical Research," *Social Indicators Research* 75 (2006). Of course, our choice still necessitates some omissions: In focusing solely on Europe, we leave out North American discourse on social cohesion, particularly prominent in Canada and in focusing on supra-national institutions, we largely ignore nation state level discourse. One consequence of this is that we see less explicit discussion of problems of multiculturalism and immigration.

2. Regina Berger-Schmitt, "Considering Social Cohesion in Quality of Life Assessments: Concept and Measurement," *Social Indicators Research* 58 (2002): 404.

3. Colin Ball, *Bridging the Gulf: Improving Social Cohesion in Europe—the Work of the European Foundation for the Improvement of Living and Working Conditions, 1984–1993* (Dublin: European Foundation for the Improvement of Living and Working Conditions, 1994), 1.

4. EU, *Treaty on European Union* (1992), Article 130a.
5. EU, *The Porto Declaration* (2021), 1.
6. EU, *Cohesion as an Overall Value of the European Union* (2021), 11.
7. EU, *Cohesion as an Overall Value*, 14.
8. EU, *Cohesion as an Overall Value*, 15.
9. EU, *Cohesion as an Overall Value*, 15.
10. EU, *Cohesion as an Overall Value*, 102.
11. Cf. EU, *Growth, Competitiveness, Employment: The Challenges and Ways forward into the 21st Century* (1994), 150.

12. EU, *Growth, Competitiveness, Employment*, 16.
13. EU, *Growth, Competitiveness, Employment*, 108.
14. EU, *Growth, Competitiveness, Employment*, 150.
15. EU, *Growth, Competitiveness, Employment*, 16.
16. EU, *Growth, Competitiveness, Employment*, 15.
17. EU, *Growth, Competitiveness, Employment*, 3.
18. EU, *European Social Policy: A Way forward for the Union* (1994), 1.
19. EU, *European Social Policy*, 4.
20. EU, *European Social Policy*, 5.
21. EU, *European Social Policy*, 37.
22. EU, *Unity, Solidarity, Diversity for Europe, Its People and Its Territory: Second Report on Economic and Social Cohesion* (2001), 23.
23. EU, *Lisbon European Council 23 and 24 March 2000: Presidency Conclusions* (2000), part I/5.
24. EU, *Lisbon European Council 23 and 24 March 2000*, part I/24.
25. EU, *Lisbon European Council 23 and 24 March 2000*, part I/31–32.
26. EU, *Communication from the Commission on the Social Agenda* (2005), 6.
27. EU, *European Council Brussels 22 and 23 March 2005: Presidency Conclusions* (2005), 10. The call for more "clear and measurable" policy priorities can be also understood as motivated by a critical awareness of some EU policymakers that "even with the present high ambitions, policies for social cohesion in EU Member States have not succeeded in arresting poverty and unemployment" (EU, *Opinion of the European Economic and Social Committee on Social Cohesion: Fleshing Out a European Social Model* [2006], 2.3.4.).
28. EU, *First Report on Economic and Social Cohesion* (1996), 14.
29. EU, *First Report*, 13.
30. EU, *First Report*, 127.
31. EU, *Europe 2020: A European Strategy for Smart, Sustainable and Inclusive Growth* (2010), 27.
32. Cf. EU, *'Laeken' Indicators: Detailed Calculation Methodology* (2003).
33. EU, *Building the Knowledge Society: Social and Human Capital Interactions* (2003), 2.
34. EU, *Building the Knowledge Society*, 37.
35. EU, *Building the Knowledge Society*, 18.
36. EU, *Building the Knowledge Society*, 52.
37. EU, *Social and Human Capital in the Knowledge Society: Learning, Work, Social Cohesion and Gender* (2003), 3–4.
38. EU, *Europe 2020*, i.
39. EU, *Europe 2020*, 16.
40. EU, *Towards Social Investment for Growth and Cohesion: Including Implementing the European Social Fund 2014–2020* (2013), 2–3.
41. EU, *Towards Social Investment for Growth and Cohesion*, 8.
42. EU, *Towards Social Investment for Growth and Cohesion*, 8.
43. EU, *Towards Social Investment for Growth and Cohesion*, 22.
44. EU, *Towards Social Investment for Growth and Cohesion*, 21.

45. EU, *Treaty on European Union* (2007), Article 2, No 1.

46. EU, *Opportunities, Access and Solidarity: Towards a New Social Vision for 21st Century Europe* (2007), 3.

47. EU, *Opportunities, Access and Solidarity*, 6–7.

48. EU, *Opportunities, Access and Solidarity*, 7.

49. EU, *Cohesion as an Overall Value*, 5.

50. EU, *Cohesion as an Overall Value*, 99.

51. EU, *Cohesion as an Overall Value*, 101.

52. The Council of Europe—not to be confused with the EU's European Council—is an international organization, based in Strasbourg, which was created in 1949 and now includes forty-six European countries. Its mission is to promote democracy, human rights, and the rule of law. It is home to the European Convention on Human Rights and the European Court of Human Rights. See https://www.coe.int/en/web/about-us.

53. CoE, *Human Dignity and Social Exclusion: Causes and Prevention within Europe* (1994), 3.

54. CoE, *Human Dignity and Social Exclusion*, 3–4.

55. CoE, *Summary of the Project Human Dignity and Social Exclusion* (1998), 1.

56. CoE, *Summary of the Project Human Dignity and Social Exclusion*, 1.

57. CoE, *Second Summit of Heads of State and Government: Final Declaration and Action Plan* (1997), part I, 3.

58. CoE, *Second Summit of Heads of State and Government*, part I, 2.

59. CoE, *Fighting Social Exclusion and Strengthening Social Cohesion in Europe* (1998), 2.

60. CoE, *Fighting Social Exclusion*, 2.

61. CoE, *Strategy for Social Cohesion* (2000), 7.

62. CoE, *Strategy for Social Cohesion*, 9.

63. CoE, *Strategy for Social Cohesion*, 8.

64. CoE, *Strategy for Social Cohesion*, 3–10.

65. CoE, *Strategy for Social Cohesion*, 6.

66. CoE, *Strategy for Social Cohesion*, 7.

67. CoE, *Revised Strategy for Social Cohesion* (2004), 2.

68. CoE, *Revised Strategy for Social Cohesion*, 3.

69. CoE, *Revised Strategy for Social Cohesion*, 4.

70. CoE, *Revised Strategy for Social Cohesion*, 5.

71. CoE, *Revised Strategy for Social Cohesion*, 7.

72. CoE, *Revised Strategy for Social Cohesion*, 8.

73. CoE, *Fighting Social Exclusion*, 3.

74. CoE, *Revised Strategy for Social Cohesion*, 11. Regarding concrete policy steps towards the goal, the *Revised Strategy* emphasizes the need to take measures across various fields of social policy, such as social protection, employment, housing, health, or education. In this respect it refers to the *Revised European Code of Social Security* and the *Revised European Social Charter* as a source for policy guidance.

75. CoE, *New Strategy and Council of Europe Action Plan for Social Cohesion* (2010), 2.

76. CoE, *New Strategy*, 8.

77. CoE, *Compilation of Replies to the Questions on Developments since the Previous Plenary Meeting* (2017), 84.

78. CoE, *New Strategy*, 2.

79. CoE, *New Strategy*, 8.

80. CoE, *New Strategy*, 4.

81. CoE, *New Strategy*, 8.

82. Surprisingly, the document does not touch on the question of social and economic disparities between various states in Europe, which is perhaps why it does not problematize the cumulative view of social cohesion in Europe, a view which is far from self-evident.

83. CoE, *New Strategy*, 4.

84. CoE, *New Strategy*, 2.

85. CoE, *New Strategy*, 2.

86. CoE, *Social Cohesion: A New Horizon for 21st Century Europe* (2021), 1.

87. CoE, *European Committee for Social Cohesion* (2021), 44.

88. Pierre Dardot and Christian Laval, *The New Way of the World: On Neoliberal Society*, trans. Gregory Elliott (London: Verso, 2013), 301–2.

89. Dobbernack, *The Politics of Social Cohesion in Germany, France and the United Kingdom* (Basingstoke: Palgrave Macmillan, 2014), 175.

90. Ben Fine, *Theories of Social Capital: Researchers Behaving Badly* (London: Pluto, 2010), 4.

91. Francesco Laruffa, "Studying the Relationship between Social Policy Promotion and Neoliberalism: The Case of Social Investment," *New Political Economy* 27, no. 3 (2022): 13.

92. Dobbernack, *The Politics of Social Cohesion*, 177.

93. Similarly, the language of inclusion divorced from that of justice can lead to its own disciplinary and coercive approaches. See Suzanne Fitzpatrick and Anwen Jones, "Pursuing Social Justice or Social Cohesion? Coercion in Street Homelessness Policies in England," *Journal of Social Policy* 3, no. 3 (2005): 389–406.

94. Andrea Cornwall, "Introductory Overview—Buzzwords and Fuzzwords: Deconstructing Development Discourse," in *Deconstructing Development Discourse: Buzzwords and Fuzzwords*, ed. Andrea Cornwall and Deborah Eade (Bourton on Dunsmore: Practical Action Publishing, 2010), 1.

95. Deborah Eade, "Preface," in *Deconstructing Development Discourse: Buzzwords and Fuzzwords*, ed. Andrea Cornwall and Deborah Eade (Bourton on Dunsmore: Practical Action Publishing, 2010), viii.

96. Guy Standing, "Social Protection," in *Deconstructing Development Discourse: Buzzwords and Fuzzwords*, ed. Andrea Cornwall and Deborah Eade (Bourton on Dunsmore: Practical Action Publishing, 2010), 65.

97. Thomas Maloutas and Maro Pantelidou Malouta, "The Glass Menagerie of Urban Governance and Social Cohesion: Concepts and Stakes / Concepts as Stakes," *International Journal of Urban and Regional Research* 28, no. 2 (2004): 452.

98. Dobbernack, *The Politics of Social Cohesion*, 49–50.

99. Gilbert Rist, "Development as a Buzzword," in *Deconstructing Development Discourse: Buzzwords and Fuzzwords*, ed. Andrea Cornwall and Deborah Eade (Bourton on Dunsmore: Practical Action Publishing, 2010), 20.
100. Eade, "Preface," p. ix.
101. Cornwall, "Introductory Overview," 2.

CHAPTER 4

1. CoE, *Strategies for Social Development and Social Cohesion in the Euro-Mediterranean Region* (2002), 10.
2. CoE, *Strategies for Social Development and Social Cohesion*, 24.
3. EU-LAC, *Declaration of Guadalajara* (2004), 6.
4. EU-LAC, *Declaration of Guadalajara*, 6.
5. EU-LAC, *Declaration of Guadalajara*, 7–8.
6. EU-LAC, *Declaration of Guadalajara*, 7.
7. For example, CARI, *Social Cohesion, Global Governance and the Future of Politics: Understanding and Fostering Social Cohesion* (2018); Asian Development Bank, *Maintaining Social Cohesion in the People's Republic of China in the New Era* (2019); USAID, *Resilience Rapid Learning Brief: Harnessing Local Sources of Social Cohesion in Niger* (2021); USAID, *Social Cohesion: Directions for Policy Development in Luhansk Oblast* (2021); German Development Institute, *Social Cohesion: A New Definition and a Proposal for Its Measurement in Africa* (2021); International Organisation for Migration, *The Power of "Contact": Designing, Facilitating and Evaluating Social Mixing Activities to Strengthen Migrant Integration and Social Cohesion Between Migrants and Local Communities* (2021); World Economic Forum, *Engaging Citizens for Inclusive Futures: Rebuilding Social Cohesion and Trust through Citizen Dialogues* (2021); German Society for International Collaboration, *Contextualizing Social Cohesion for Different Sectors and Actors in the Refugee Response in Turkey* (2022); Mercy Corps, *Strengthening Social Cohesion for Violence Prevention: Ten Lessons for Policymakers and Practitioners* (2022); Price Waterhouse Cooper Network, *Rebuilding Social Cohesion Is an Essential Contributor to Economic Development in South Africa* (2022); Inter-American Development Bank, *Trust—The Key to Social Cohesion and Growth in Latin America and the Caribbean* (2022).
8. Thus, we do not focus in as much detail on the World Bank—a significant global actor—simply because it follows a similar trajectory to that of the OECD, with social cohesion emerging first as closely connected to economic growth and 'room for manoeuvre' (e.g., World Bank Group, *On "Good" Politicians and "Bad" Policies: Social Cohesion, Institutions, and Growth* [2000]) and gradually 'thickening' towards incorporating concepts of sustainability. Increasingly it sees social cohesion as part of a package of goods with "both intrinsic and instrumental value" (World Bank Group, *Social Sustainability in Development: Meeting the Challenges of the 21st Century*, [2023] 2).

9. Most obviously in their size, with OECD having significantly fewer members, rooted heavily in the Global North, and in their historical mandate, with the OECD being originally oriented towards economic cooperation and the UN mandated to maintain international peace and security.

10. These organizations tend to draw on the same ideas: see, for example, Francesco Burchi, Markus Loewe, Daniele Malerba, and Julia Leininger, "Disentangling the Relationship Between Social Protection and Social Cohesion: Introduction to the Special Issue," *The European Journal of Development Research* 34, no. 3 (2022): 1195–215. One of the authors also provided the German International Development Agency's account of social cohesion we discuss below: see Julia Leininger, Francesco Burchi, Charlotte Fiedler, Karina Moss, Daniel Nowack, Armin von Schiller, Christoph Sommer, Christoph Strupat, and Sebastian Ziaja, *Social Cohesion: A New Definition and a Proposal for Its Measurement in Africa* (Bonn: Deutsches Institut für Entwicklungspolitik, 2021). It is also worth mentioning that the OECD and the UN often play the role of a reference point for these organizations and think-tanks.

11. OECD, *Beyond 2000: The New Social Policy Agenda: Socio-economic Change and Social Policy Issues* (1996), 6–7.

12. OECD, *Beyond 2000: Summary* (1997), 7.

13. OECD, *Beyond 2000: Summary*, 4.

14. OECD, *Beyond 2000: Summary*, 6.

15. OECD, *Societal Cohesion and the Globalising Economy: What Does the Future Hold?* (1997), 3.

16. OECD, *Societal Cohesion*, 19.

17. OECD, *Societal Cohesion*, 3.

18. OECD, *Societal Cohesion*, 3.

19. OECD, *Societal Cohesion*, 7–8.

20. OECD, *Societal Cohesion*, 13.

21. OECD, *Societal Cohesion*, 18.

22. OECD, *Societal Cohesion*, 21.

23. OECD, *Societal Cohesion*, 23.

24. OECD, *Societal Cohesion*, 20.

25. OECD, *Societal Cohesion*, 21. The relationship between growth and social cohesion was restated in a more convoluted way in the document *Human Capital Investment*, which connects the need for human capital investment—investing in the knowledge and skills of workers—with strategies to "foster social cohesion" (OECD, *Human Capital Investment: An International Comparison* [1998], 8). In this framing, the non-economic "spin-off" benefits of human capital investment are in turn expected to "feed back into economic well-being" (OECD, *Human Capital Investment*, 66). Thus, investing in human capital aids social cohesion, but at the same time, "For growth and prosperity to be sustainable, social cohesion is required; here too, the role of human capital is vital" (OECD, *Human Capital Investment*, 91). In these documents, then, social cohesion remains vaguely characterized as a "strong social fabric" and as the opposite of "social fragmentation" (OECD, *Societal Cohesion*, 1997, p. 7).

26. Amartya Sen, *The Standard of Living* (Cambridge: Cambridge University Press, 1987).

27. OECD, *The Well-Being of Nations: The Role of Human and Social Capital* (2001), 10.
28. OECD, *Interim Report on the OECD Three-Year Project on Sustainable Development* (1999), 2.
29. Jane Jenson, *Mapping Social Cohesion: The State of Canadian Research*, Study No. F/03 (Ottawa: Canadian Policy Research Networks, 1998).
30. OECD, *Perspectives on Global Development 2012: Social Cohesion in a Shifting World* (2011), 53.
31. OECD, *Perspectives on Global Development 2012*, 51.
32. OECD, *Perspectives on Global Development 2012*, 15.
33. OECD, *Perspectives on Global Development 2012*, 53.
34. OECD, *Perspectives on Global Development 2012*, 53–54.
35. OECD, *Perspectives on Global Development 2012*, 55.
36. OECD, *Perspectives on Global Development 2012*, 55.
37. Joseph E. Stiglitz, Amartya Sen, and Jean-Paul Fitoussi, *Report by the Commission on the Measurement of Economic Performance and Social Progress* (2009).
38. OECD, *Perspectives on Global Development 2012*, 57.
39. OECD, *Perspectives on Global Development 2012*, 17.
40. OECD, *Perspectives on Global Development 2012*, 57.
41. OECD, *Perspectives on Global Development 2012*, 60.
42. OECD, *Perspectives on Global Development 2012*, 17.
43. OECD, *Perspectives on Global Development 2012*, 51.
44. Cited in OECD, *Perspectives on Global Development 2012*, 57–58.
45. OECD, *Perspectives on Global Development 2012*, 61.
46. OECD, *Perspectives on Global Development 2012*, 25. The Concept Note on OECD Social Cohesion Policy Reviews builds on this, arguing that "new resources from improved economic performance can be used to broaden the fiscal space for a more ambitious social agenda and inclusive growth" (OECD, *Perspectives on Global Development 2012*, 1) and framing social cohesion largely in terms of 'inclusion' through employment and entrepreneurship.
47. OECD, *Social Cohesion Policy Review of Viet Nam* (2014), 33.
48. OECD, *Peer Review: An OECD Tool for Co-operation and Change* (2003).
49. See, for example, Union of Education Norway, *From Inspiration to Uniformity? 20 Years of OECD in the Field of Early Childhood Education and Care* (2020).
50. Duncan Green, "Social Cohesion—There's a Lot More to It Than the OECD Version" (Oxfam, 2012). https://frompoverty.oxfam.org.uk/social-cohesion-a-lot-more-interesting-than-the-oecd-makes-out/. Accessed May 26, 2023.
51. UN-ECLAC, *Social Cohesion: Inclusion and a Sense of Belonging in Latin America and the Caribbean* (2007). It is worth noting that the preparation of this document was co-sponsored by the Spanish Agency for International Cooperation.
52. UN-ECLAC, *Social Cohesion*, 20.
53. UN-ECLAC, *Social Cohesion*, 13.
54. UN-ECLAC, *Social Cohesion*, 18.
55. UN-ECLAC, *Social Cohesion*, 18.
56. UN-ECLAC, *Social Cohesion*, 27.

57. UN-ECLAC, *Social Cohesion*, 109.
58. UN-ECLAC, *Social Cohesion*, 126.
59. UN-ECLAC, *Social Cohesion*, 126.
60. UN-ECLAC, *Social Cohesion*, 132.
61. UN-ECLAC, *Social Cohesion*, 143.
62. UN-ECLAC, *Social Cohesion*, 156.
63. UNDP, "About Us," https://www.undp.org/about-us, accessed May 26, 2023.
64. UNDP, *Community Security and Social Cohesion: Towards a UNDP Approach* (2009), 14.
65. UNDP, *Community Security and Social Cohesion*, 14.
66. Regina Berger-Schmitt, *Social Cohesion as an Aspect of the Quality of Societies*, 4.
67. UNDP, *Community Security and Social Cohesion*, 14.
68. UNDP, *Community Security and Social Cohesion*, 14.
69. UNDP, *Promoting Social Cohesion in the Arab Region: Project Document* (2014). The program was realized between 2014 and 2017, with a budget over USD$14 million.
70. UNDP, *Promoting Social Cohesion in the Arab Region*, 4.
71. Jenson, *Mapping Social Cohesion*.
72. UNDP, *Promoting Social Cohesion in the Arab Region*, 3.
73. UNDP, *Promoting Social Cohesion in the Arab Region*, 8.
74. UNDP, *Promoting Social Cohesion in the Arab Region*, 9.
75. UNDP, *Developing a Social Cohesion Index for the Arab Region* (2017), 16. It is worth noting that the document makes a telling point with respect to the multiplicity of existing definitions of social cohesion: "While definitions of social cohesion remained elusive, different stakeholders adopted conceptions of social cohesion that addressed their specific goals and needs (e.g., OECD, World Bank, Council of Europe, UNDP, UNESCO). The elasticity of the social cohesion concept highlights its political nature, since the selection of one approach over another reflects a 'political choice' about the means one would consider for fostering social cohesion." (UNDP, *Developing a Social Cohesion Index for the Arab Region*, 13).
76. UNDP-USAID, *Predicting Peace: The Social Cohesion and Reconciliation Index as a Tool for Conflict Transformation* (2015), 28.
77. UNDP, *Towards a Measurement of Social Cohesion for Africa* (2016), 8.
78. UNDP, *Towards a Measurement of Social Cohesion for Africa*, 9.
79. UNDP-USAID, *Predicting Peace*, 22.
80. UNDP-USAID, *Predicting Peace*, 62.
81. UNDP, *Towards a Measurement of Social Cohesion for Africa*, 34.
82. UNDP, *Strengthening Social Cohesion: Conceptual Framing and Programming Implications* (2020), 16.
83. UNDP, *Strengthening Social Cohesion*, 16, fn. 7.
84. UNDP, *Strengthening Social Cohesion*, 39.
85. UNDP, *Strengthening Social Cohesion*, 18.
86. Chan et al., "Reconsidering Social Cohesion," 281.
87. UN-ECLAC, 2007, *Social Cohesion*, 18.

88. UNDP, *Social Cohesion Framework: Social Cohesion for Stronger Communities* (2015), 8.
89. UNDP, *Social Cohesion Framework*, 14.
90. UNDP, *Promoting Social Cohesion in the Arab Region*, 9.
91. UNDP, *Promoting Social Cohesion in the Arab Region*, 9.
92. Leininger et al., *Social Cohesion*, Abstract.
93. Martin Doornbos, *Social Research and Policy in the Development Arena* (Basingstoke: Palgrave Macmillan, 2015), 211.
94. Gilbert Rist, *The History of Development: From Western Origins to Global Faith*, trans. Patrick Camiller (New York: Zed Books, 2008), 254.
95. Mark Duffield, *Development, Security and Unending War: Governing the World of Peoples* (Cambridge: Polity Press, 2007), 228.
96. Juan Telleria, *Deconstructing Human Development: From the Washington Consensus to the 2030 Agenda* (New York: Routledge, 2021), 10.
97. Telleria, *Deconstructing Human Development*, 28.
98. Telleria, *Deconstructing Human Development*, 11.
99. Rist, *The History of Development*, 255.
100. Mike Savage, *The Return of Inequality: Social Change and the Weight of the Past* (Cambridge, MA: Harvard University Press, 2021), 116.
101. Savage, *The Return of Inequality*, 115. Miguel Pickard likewise stresses the relationship between quantitative indicators and the need to measure 'success' (see Miguel Pickard, "Reflections on Relationships: The Nature of Partnership According to Five NGOs in Southern Mexico," in *Deconstructing Development Discourse: Buzzwords and Fuzzwords*, ed. Andrea Cornwall and Deborah Eade [Bourton on Dunsmore: Practical Action Publishing, 2010], 141).
102. Cf. Jeremy Rappleye, Hikaru Komatsu, Yukiko Uchida, Kuba Krys, and Hazel Markus, "'Better Policies for Better Lives'?: Constructive Critique of the OECD's (Mis)measure of Student Well-being," *Journal of Education Policy* 35, no. 2 (2019): 258–82. DOI: 10.1080/02680939.2019.1576923. Katherine Selena Taylor, Sheri Longboat, and Rupert Quentin Grafton, "Whose Rules? A Water Justice Critique of the OECD's 12 Principles on Water Governance," *Water* 11, no. 4, 809 (2019). DOI: 10.3390/w11040809. János Allenbach-Ammann, "How Rich Countries Profit from the OECD Tax Deal," (Euractive), https://www.euractiv.com/section/economy-jobs/news/how-rich-countries-profit-from-the-oecd-tax-deal/, accessed May 26, 2023.
103. UNDP, *Social Cohesion Framework*, 5.
104. UNDP, *Social Cohesion Framework*, 7.
105. UNDP, *Social Cohesion Framework*, 9.
106. UNDP, *Social Cohesion Framework*, 10. It is worth mentioning that this UNDP development project comes shortly after major humanitarian crises in Myanmar that were linked with inter-communal violence and forced displacement of hundreds of thousand people.
107. UNDP, *Strengthening Social Cohesion*, 21.
108. UNDP, *Strengthening Social Cohesion*, 21.
109. UNDP, *Strengthening Social Cohesion*, 25.

110. Though this belief is not without its own problems, see, for example, the critique of country ownership.

111. Likewise, the authors of the Social Cohesion Radar note that "that the major languages of the various Asian regions lack a direct linguistic equivalent to the term social cohesion," but do not see this as a barrier to applying their conceptualization to Asia or a reason to reflect on whether its meaning might be less stable even in European contexts. Jan Delhey, Klaus Boehnke, Georgi Dragolov, Zsófia Ignácz, Mandi Larsen, Jan Lorenz, and Michael Koch, "Social Cohesion and Its Correlates: A Comparison of Western and Asian Societies," *Comparative Sociology* 17, no. 3–4 (2018): 431.

112. UN-ECLAC, *Social Cohesion and Inclusive Social Development in Latin America*, 8.

CHAPTER 5

1. Milton Friedman, *Capitalism and Freedom* (Chicago: University of Chicago Press, 2002 [1962]), xvi.

2. Wendy Brown, *Undoing the Demos: Neoliberalism's Stealth Revolution* (New York: Zone Books, 2015).

3. William Davies, *The Limits of Neoliberalism: Authority, Sovereignty and the Logic of Competition* (London: Sage Publications, 2014), 4.

4. Davies, *The Limits of Neoliberalism*, 167. This pushes somewhat beyond the earlier, pre-1980s, framework of neoliberalism, while still "remain[ing] technocratic, with the socio-economic telos captured in metrics of 'wellbeing,' 'resilience' and 'sustainability,' and the means of pursuing these goals remain organized in terms of incentives, choices, strategies and individual agents" (Davies, *The Limits of Neoliberalism*, 171).

5. Pierre Bourdieu and Loic Wacquant, "NewLiberalSpeak: Notes on the New Planetary Vulgate," *Radical Philosophy* 105 (2001): 3.

6. German Institute of Development and Sustainability, "Concepts," *Social Cohesion Hub*, https://www.socialcohesion.info/concepts. Accessed May 29, 2023.

7. J. Kasper Gregersen, "Assessing the Glue That Holds Society Together: Social Cohesion Arguments in Liberal Democracy," *Tidsskrift for Medier, Erkendelse Og Formidling* 1, no. 2 (2013): 89.

8. See, for example, "because of its recognized importance in nation building, a focus on measuring social cohesion has gained traction in recent years" (UNDP, *Social Cohesion Framework*, 12.)

9. Willem H. Buiter, "'Country Ownership': A Term Whose Time Has Gone," in *Deconstructing Development Discourse: Buzzwords and Fuzzwords*, ed. Andrea Cornwall and Deborah Eade (Bourton on Dunsmore: Practical Action Publishing, 2010), 224.

10. This would be to offer a 'critical theory' in the strong (and often controversial) sense of the term. See, for example, Raymond Geuss, *The Idea of a Critical*

Theory: Habermas and the Frankfurt School (Cambridge: Cambridge University Press, 1981).

11. See Andrea Cornwall and Karen Brock, "What Do Buzzwords Do for Development Policy? A Critical Look at 'Participation,' 'Empowerment' and 'Poverty Reduction,'" *Third World Quarterly* 26, no. 7 (2005): 1056: "If words make worlds, struggles over meaning are not just about semantics: they gain a very real material dimension."

12. To anticipate an objection: none of this should be read as saying that words directly *determine* our reality, or that they are the *only* things that matter.

13. Here are two examples of this 'broad' approach. Robert Paul Wolff suggests that the invocation of tolerance in 1960s United States was ideological because it took for granted the existing structure of social groups, arguing "pluralism is not explicitly a philosophy of privilege or injustice—it is a philosophy of equality and justice whose *concrete application* supports inequality by ignoring the existence of certain legitimate social groups" (Robert Paul Wolff, Barrington Moore Jr., and Herbert Marcuse, *A Critique of Pure Tolerance* [London: Cape Editions, 1969], 52). In a different key, Lorna Finlayson argues that the dominant form taken by contemporary political philosophy tends unduly to delegitimize and exclude critical perspectives in a way that takes for granted certain aspects of the *status quo*. Neither case depends on—or rules out—a specific story about *how* this happens, but rather points to the fact that it *does* happen. As Finlayson observes, "the idea that certain of the distortions of thought to which we are subject can be functionally explained, including in terms of the interests they further, is a very generally applicable one—as witnessed by a whole range of phenomena from wishful thinking, to the power of advertising, to the power of love" (Lorna Finlayson, *The Political Is Political: Conformity and the Illusion of Dissent in Contemporary Political Philosophy* [Lanham: Rowman & Littlefield, 2015], 169).

14. For example, "social cohesion is a necessary component for building resilience and improving longterm well-being outcomes" (USAID, *Harnessing Local Sources of Social Cohesion in Niger*, 4); "Strengthening social cohesion is an important component of shaping state policies of sustainable peacebuilding, socio-economic development, national unity and social resilience" (USAID, *Social Cohesion: Directions for Policy Development in Luhansk Oblast*, 4); "Social cohesion makes communities and states more resilient in the face of crises and facilitates change processes that benefit everyone" (Julia Leininger, Francesco Burchi, Charlotte Fiedler, Karina Moss, Daniel Nowack, Armin von Schiller, Christoph Sommer, Christoph Strupat, and Sebastian Ziaja, *Social Cohesion: A New Definition and a Proposal for Its Measurement in Africa* [Bonn: Deutsches Institut für Entwicklungspolitik, 2021], 1); "The resilience of a society is dependent on high levels of social cohesion" (World Economic Forum. *Engaging Citizens for Inclusive Futures: Rebuilding Social Cohesion and Trust through Citizen Dialogues.* 2021, 3).

15. See Peer Illner, *Disasters and Social Reproduction: Crisis Response between the State and Community* (London: Pluto Press, 2020), chap. 2; Mark Neocleous, "Resisting Resilience," *Radical Philosophy* 178 (2013), https://www.radicalphilosophy.com/commentary/resisting-resilience.

16. Ben Fine, "Social Capital," in *Deconstructing Development Discourse: Buzzwords and Fuzzwords*, ed. Andrea Cornwall and Deborah Eade (Bourton on Dunsmore: Practical Action Publishing, 2010), 132.

17. Gilbert Rist, "Development as a Buzzword," in *Deconstructing Development Discourse: Buzzwords and Fuzzwords*, ed. Andrea Cornwall and Deborah Eade (Bourton on Dunsmore: Practical Action Publishing, 2010), 21.

18. Neera Chandhoke, "Civil Society," in *Deconstructing Development Discourse: Buzzwords and Fuzzwords*, ed. Andrea Cornwall and Deborah Eade (Bourton on Dunsmore: Practical Action Publishing, 2010), 176.

19. Chandhoke, "Civil Society," 182.

20. Chandhoke, "Civil Society," 183.

21. Walter B. Gallie, "Essentially Contested Concepts," *Proceedings of the Aristotelian Society* 56, no. 1 (1956): 169. There are limits to applying Gallie's approach. It depends on two important conditions: first, that the concept is derived from "an original exemplar whose authority is acknowledged by all the contestant users of the concept"; and, second, that the "continuous competition for acknowledgement as between the contestant users of the concept, enables the original exemplar's achievement to be sustained and/or developed in optimum fashion." As we have discussed, there are certainly attempts to locate social cohesion as part of a longer tradition, for example representing it as an extension of the language of solidarity and fraternity, or even some vision of the European ideal. At the same time, however, we have seen how there is disagreement—for example, in accounts that are happy to represent totalitarian regimes as socially cohesive. Moreover, even if there were agreement on exemplars, it remains unclear whether—or how—continued dispute over social cohesion's meaning might help sustain and develop them.

22. As discussed in chapter 3, the Council of Europe did at one point refrain from offering a definition, but this quickly gave way.

23. Paul Bernard, *Social Cohesion: A Critique*, Discussion Paper No. F/09 (Ottawa: Canadian Policy Research Networks, 1999), 24.

24. Thomas Maloutas and Maro Pantelidou Malouta, "The Glass Menagerie of Urban Governance and Social Cohesion: Concepts and Stakes/ Concepts as Stakes," *International Journal of Urban and Regional Research* 28, no. 2 (2004): 463.

25. If we accept the previous section's characterization of social cohesion as an ideological concept, this might be a way of representing it as a *utopian* concept, in Mannheim's sense of ideas that are "incongruous with the state of reality within which it occurs" and which "when they pass over into conduct, tend to shatter, either partially or wholly, the order of things prevailing at the time" (Karl Mannheim, *Ideology and Utopia* [London: Routledge and Kegan Paul, 1960], 173).

26. Cornwall and Brock, "What Do Buzzwords Do for Development Policy?" 1047.

27. Cornwall and Brock, "What Do Buzzwords Do for Development Policy?" 1057.

28. Georgi Dragolov, Zsófia S. Ignácz, Jan Lorenz, Jan Delhey, Klaus Boehnke, and Kai Unzicker, *Social Cohesion in the Western World: What Holds Societies Together: Insights from the Social Cohesion Radar* (Dordrecht: Springer, 2016), 63.

29. See UN-ECLAC, *Social Cohesion and Inclusive Social Development in Latin America: A Proposal for an Era of Uncertainties* (2022), 8.

30. Mike Savage, *The Return of Inequality: Social Change and the Weight of the Past* (Cambridge, MA: Harvard University Press, 2021).

31. This context is explicitly noted by the director of the Bertelsmann Stiftung's Living Values Program in his introduction to Dragolov et al., *Social Cohesion in the Western World*, x. Another central figure in putting inequality back on the agenda, Joseph Stiglitz, plays an important role in the OECD literature analyzed in the previous chapter.

32. Cited in Savage, *The Return of Inequality*, 1.

33. World Economic Forum. *The Global Risks Report 2022: 17th Edition* (Geneva: World Economic Forum, 2022).

34. Savage, *The Return of Inequality*, 79.

35. Savage, *The Return of Inequality*, 75.

36. Savage, *The Return of Inequality*, 227.

37. To give just a couple of contemporary examples, Anne Phillips stresses an understanding of equality as "something *we make happen* in those moments when we assert ourselves as equals" which "sometimes takes the form of committing oneself to the equality of others and sometimes of claiming it for oneself" (Anne Phillips, *Unconditional Equals* [Princeton: Princeton University Press, 2021], 112). Joan Tronto offers another perspective on equality with respect to the allocation of caring responsibilities in a democratic society in *Caring Democracy: Markets, Equality, and Justice* (New York: New York University Press, 2013).

38. See, in this context, Smith and Kulynych's critique of similar arguments around social capital: "for Putnam to conceptualize the solidarity in 'Solidarity Forever' as a form of social capital makes a mockery of the song's aspiration that working-class solidarity can help birth a new world not plagued by capitalist economic, political, and social relations." Stephen S. Smith and Jessica Kulynych, "It May Be Social, But Why Is It Capital? The Social Construction of Social Capital and the Politics of Language," *Politics and Society* 30, no.1 (2002): 149–86.

39. See Dan Swain, Petr Urban, Catherine Malabou, and Petr Kouba, eds., *Unchaining Solidarities: On Mutual Aid and Anarchism with Catherine Malabou* (Lanham: Rowman & Littlefield, 2021). On the idea of prefigurative strategies see Paul Raekstad and Sofa Saio Gradin, *Prefigurative Politics: Building Tomorrow Today* (Cambridge: Polity, 2020); Matthijs van de Sande, *Prefigurative Democracy: Protest, Social Movements and the Political Institution of Society* (Edinburgh: University of Edinburgh Press, 2022); Lara Monticelli, "On the Necessity of Prefigurative Politics," *Thesis Eleven* 167, no. 1 (2021): 99 118. https://doi.org/10.1177/07255136211056992.

40. See Jeremy Gilbert, "An Aesthetics of Solidarity: Collective Becoming After Neoliberalism," in *Crisis and Communitas*, ed. Dorota Sajewska and Małgorzata Sugiera (Abingdon: Routledge, 2023), 21–39.

41. Dean Spade, *Mutual Aid: Building Solidarity During This Crisis and the Next* (London and New York: Verso, 2020).

42. Rhiannon Firth, *Disaster Anarchy: Mutual Aid and Radical Action* (London: Pluto Press, 2022); Peer Illner, *Disasters and Social Reproduction: Crisis Response between the State and Community* (London: Pluto Press, 2020).

43. See, for example, Aaron Jaffe, *Social Reproduction Theory and the Socialist Horizon* (London: Pluto Press, 2020).

44. Peter Kropotkin, *Mutual Aid: A Factor of Evolution* (London: Freedom Press, 2009 [1902]).

45. Rowan Williams, *Solidarity: Necessary Fiction or Metaphysical Given. Third Gillian Rose Memorial Lecture* (Kingston: CRMEP Books, 2023).

46. Tamara Caraus and Elena Paris, eds., *Migration, Protest Movements and the Politics of Resistance* (New York: Routledge, 2019); Natasha King, *No Borders: The Politics of Immigration Control and Resistance* (London: Zed Books, 2016).

47. Taking solidarity seriously as a political value is a key element of several recent proposals for a political theory of care. Cf. Tronto, *Caring Democracy*; or Kathleen Lynch, *Care and Capitalism* (Cambridge: Polity, 2022).

48. Juan Telleria, *Deconstructing Human Development: From the Washington Consensus to the 2030 Agenda* (New York: Routledge, 2021).

49. Arturo Escobar, *Pluriversal Politics: The Real and the Possible* (Durham, NC: Duke University Press, 2020), 26.

50. See Escobar, *Pluriversal Politics*, 76–80; Roger Merino, "An Alternative to 'Alternative Development'?: Buen Vivir and Human Development in Andean Countries," *Oxford Development Studies* 44, no. 3 (2016): 271–86, http://dx.doi.org/10.1080/13600818.2016.1144733.

51. See, James D. Ingram, "Cosmopolitanism from Below: Universalism as Contestation," *Critical Horizons* 17, no. 1 (2016): 66–78; Alex Sager, "Reclaiming Cosmopolitanism Through Migrant Protests," in *Migration, Protest Movements and the Politics of Resistance*, ed. Tamara Caraus and Elena Paris (New York: Routledge, 2019), 171–85.

52. Dragolov et al., *Social Cohesion in the Western* World, 6. This focus on the common good also forms an important part of the UN-ECLAC document discussed in the previous chapter (see UN-ECLAC, *Social Cohesion and Inclusive Social Development in Latin America*, 55).

53. Alasdair MacIntyre, "Politics, Philosophy and the Common Good," in *The MacIntyre Reader*, ed. Kelvin Knight (South Bend: University of Notre Dame Press, 1998), 240.

54. MacIntyre, "Politics, Philosophy and the Common Good," 240.

55. MacIntyre, "Politics, Philosophy and the Common Good," 241.

56. For example, "Social scientists are convinced that, in societies as in sports teams, cohesion represents a positive quality that brings with it a sense of resilience and a marked orientation towards the common good" (Eurofound, *Social Cohesion and Well-being in Europe* [Luxembourg: Publications Office of the European Union, 2018], 3).

57. MacIntyre, "Politics, Philosophy and the Common Good," 243.

58. Pierre Dardot and Christian Laval, *The New Way of the World: On Neoliberal Society*, trans. Gregory Elliott (London: Verso, 2013), 188. See also Wendy Brown, *In the Ruins of Neoliberalism: The Rise of Antidemocratic Politics in the West* (New York: Columbia University Press, 2019), 62–63: "The exceptionally thin version of democracy that neoliberalism tolerates is thus detached from political freedom,

political equality, and power sharing by citizens, from legislation aimed at the common good, from any notion of a public interest exceeding protection of individual liberties and security, and from cultures of participation."

59. Donatella Della Porta, *How Social Movements Can Save Democracy: Democratic Innovations from Below* (Cambridge: Polity, 2020).

60. Max Koch, Jayeon Lindellee, and Johanna Alkan Olsson, "Beyond the Growth Imperative and Neoliberal Doxa: Expanding Alternative Societal Spaces through Deliberative Citizen Forums on Needs Satisfaction," *real-world economics review* 96 (2021): 168–83, http://www.paecon.net/PAEReview/issue96/Koch-et-al96.pdf.

61. Matthew Thompson, "What's So New about New Municipalism?" *Progress in Human Geography* 45, no. 2 (2021): 317–42.

62. Bonnie Honig, *Public Things: Democracy in Disrepair* (New York: Fordham University Press, 2017); Elinor Ostrom, *Governing the Commons* (Cambridge: Cambridge University Press, 2015).

63. See James C. Scott, *Seeing Like a State: How Certain Schemes to Improve the Human Condition Have Failed* (New Haven: Yale University Press, 1999) and Davina Cooper, *Feeling Like a State: Desire, Denial, and the Recasting of Authority* (Durham: Duke University Press, 2019).

Bibliography Part A
Policy Literature

Asian Development Bank. *Maintaining Social Cohesion in the People's Republic of China in the New Era.* 2019.

Ball, Colin. *Bridging the Gulf: Improving Social Cohesion in Europe — the Work of the European Foundation for the Improvement of Living and Working Conditions, 1984–1993.* Dublin: European Foundation for the Improvement of Living and Working Conditions, 1994.

CARI. *Social Cohesion, Global Governance and the Future of Politics: Understanding and Fostering Social Cohesion.* 2018.

CoE. *Compilation of Replies to the Questions on Developments since the Previous Plenary Meeting.* 2017.

CoE. *European Committee for Social Cohesion.* 2021.

CoE. *Fighting Social Exclusion and Strengthening Social Cohesion in Europe.* 1998.

CoE. *Human Dignity and Social Exclusion: Causes and Prevention within Europe.* 1994.

CoE. *New Strategy and Council of Europe Action Plan for Social Cohesion.* 2010.

CoE. *Revised Strategy for Social Cohesion.* 2004.

CoE. *Second Summit of Heads of State and Government: Final Declaration and Action Plan.* 1997.

CoE. *Social Cohesion: A New Horizon for 21st Century Europe.* 2021.

CoE. *Strategies for Social Development and Social Cohesion in the Euro-Mediterranean Region.* 2002.

CoE. *Strategy for Social Cohesion.* 2000.

CoE. *Summary of the Project Human Dignity and Social Exclusion.* 1998.

EU. *Building the Knowledge Society: Social and Human Capital Interactions.* 2003.

EU. *Cohesion as an Overall Value of the European Union.* 2021.

EU. *Europe 2020: A European Strategy for Smart, Sustainable and Inclusive Growth.* 2010.

EU. *European Council Brussels 22 and 23 March 2005: Presidency Conclusions.* 2005.

EU. *European Social Policy: A Way forward for the Union.* 1994.

EU. *First Report on Economic and Social Cohesion.* 1996.

EU. *Growth, Competitiveness, Employment: The Challenges and Ways forward into the 21st Century.* 1994.
EU. *'Laeken' Indicators: Detailed Calculation Methodology.* 2003.
EU. *Lisbon European Council 23 and 24 March 2000: Presidency Conclusions.* 2000.
EU. *Opinion of the European Economic and Social Committee on Social Cohesion: Fleshing Out a European Social Model.* 2006.
EU. *Opportunities, Access and Solidarity: Towards a New Social Vision for 21st Century Europe.* 2007.
EU. *Social and Human Capital in the Knowledge Society: Learning, Work, Social Cohesion and Gender.* 2003.
EU. *The Porto Declaration.* 2021.
EU. *Towards Social Investment for Growth and Cohesion: Including Implementing the European Social Fund 2014–2020.* 2013.
EU. *Treaty on European Union.* 1992.
EU. *Treaty on European Union.* 2007.
EU. *Unity, Solidarity, Diversity for Europe, Its People and Its Territory: Second Report on Economic and Social Cohesion.* 2001.
EU-LAC. *Declaration of Guadalajara.* 2004.
Eurofound. *Social Cohesion and Well-Being in Europe.* Luxembourg: Publications Office of the European Union, 2018.
German Development Institute. *Social Cohesion: A New Definition and a Proposal for Its Measurement in Africa.* 2021.
German Institute of Development and Sustainability. "Concepts." Accessed May 29, 2023. https://www.socialcohesion.info/concepts.
German Society for International Collaboration. *Contextualizing Social Cohesion for Different Sectors and Actors in the Refugee Response in Turkey.* 2022.
Inter-American Development Bank. *Trust—The Key to Social Cohesion and Growth in Latin America and the Caribbean.* 2022.
International Organisation for Migration. *The Power of "Contact": Designing, Facilitating and Evaluating Social Mixing Activities to Strengthen Migrant Integration and Social Cohesion between Migrants and Local Communities.* 2021.
Mercy Corps. *Strengthening Social Cohesion for Violence Prevention: Ten Lessons for Policymakers and Practitioners.* 2022.
OECD. *Beyond 2000: Summary.* 1997.
OECD. *Beyond 2000: The New Social Policy Agenda: Socio-economic Change and Social Policy Issues.* 1996.
OECD. *Human Capital Investment: An International Comparison.* 1998.
OECD. *Interim Report on the OECD Three-Year Project on Sustainable Development.* 1999.
OECD. *Peer Review: An OECD Tool for Co-operation and Change.* 2003.
OECD. *Perspectives on Global Development 2012: Social Cohesion in a Shifting World.* 2011.
OECD. *Social Cohesion Policy Review of Viet Nam.* 2014.
OECD. *Societal Cohesion and the Globalising Economy: What Does the Future Hold?* 1997.

OECD. *The Well-Being of Nations: The Role of Human and Social Capital.* 2001.
Policy Research Initiative. *Sustaining Growth, Human Development, and Social Cohesion in a Global World.* Government of Canada, 1999.
Price Waterhouse Cooper Network. *Rebuilding Social Cohesion is an Essential Contributor to Economic Development in South Africa.* 2022.
UNDP. "About us." Accessed May 26, 2023. https://www.undp.org/about-us.
UNDP. *Community Security and Social Cohesion: Towards a UNDP Approach.* 2009.
UNDP. *Developing a Social Cohesion Index for the Arab Region.* 2017.
UNDP. *Promoting Social Cohesion in the Arab Region: Project Document.* 2014.
UNDP. *Social Cohesion Framework: Social Cohesion for Stronger Communities.* 2015.
UNDP. *Strengthening Social Cohesion: Conceptual Framing and Programming Implications.* 2020.
UNDP. *Towards a Measurement of Social Cohesion for Africa.* 2016.
UNDP-USAID. *Predicting Peace: The Social Cohesion and Reconciliation Index as a Tool for Conflict Transformation.* 2015.
UN-ECLAC. *Social Cohesion: Inclusion and a Sense of Belonging in Latin America and the Caribbean.* 2007.
UN-ECLAC. *Social Cohesion and Inclusive Social Development in Latin America: A Proposal for an Era of Uncertainties.* 2022.
USAID. *Resilience Rapid Learning Brief: Harnessing Local Sources of Social Cohesion in Niger.* 2021.
USAID. *Social Cohesion: Directions for Policy Development in Luhansk Oblast.* 2021.
World Bank Group. *On "Good" Politicians and "Bad" Policies: Social Cohesion, Institutions, and Growth.* 2000.
World Bank Group. *Social Sustainability in Development: Meeting the Challenges of the 21st Century.* 2023.
World Economic Forum. *Engaging Citizens for Inclusive Futures: Rebuilding Social Cohesion and Trust through Citizen Dialogues.* 2021.

Bibliography Part B
Research Literature

Allenbach-Ammann, János. "How Rich Countries Profit from the OECD Tax Deal." Euractive. Accessed May 26, 2023. https://www.euractiv.com/section/economy-jobs/news/how-rich-countries-profit-from-the-oecd-tax-deal./

Arneil, Barbara. *Diverse Communities: The Problem with Social Capital.* Cambridge: Cambridge University Press, 2006.

Aruqaj, Bujar. *Social Cohesion in European Societies: Conceptualising and Assessing Togetherness.* London—New York: Routledge, 2023.

Avery, E. Eileen, Joan M. Hermsen, and Danielle C. Kuhl. "Toward a Better Understanding of Perceptions of Neighbourhood Social Cohesion in Rural and Urban Places." *Social Indicators Research* 157 (2021): 523–41.

Berger-Schmitt, Regina. *Social Cohesion as an Aspect of the Quality of Societies: Concept and Measurement.* Mannheim: Center for Survey Research and Methodology, 2000.

Bernard, Paul. *Social Cohesion: A Critique*, Discussion Paper No. F/09. Ottawa: Canadian Policy Research Networks, 1999.

Bertelsmann Stiftung. *What Holds Asian Societies Together? Insights from the Social Cohesion Radar.* Verlag Bertelsmann Stiftung, 2018.

Bottoni, Gianmaria. "A Multilevel Measurement Model of Social Cohesion." *Social Indicators Research* 136, no. 3 (2018): 835–57.

Bourdieu, Pierre, and Loic Wacquant. "NewLiberalSpeak: Notes on the New Planetary Vulgate." *Radical Philosophy* 105 (2001).

Brecher, Bob. *Torture and the Ticking Time Bomb.* Oxford: Blackwell, 2007.

British Academy. *The COVID Decade: Understanding the Long-Term Societal Impacts of COVID-19.* London: The British Academy, 2021.

Broadhead, Jacqueline. *Social Cohesion in Europe: Literature Review.* The British Council, 2022. https://www.britishcouncil.org/research-policy-insight/research-reports/social-cohesion.

Brown, Wendy. *Undoing the Demos: Neoliberalism's Stealth Revolution.* New York: Zone Books, 2015.

Brown, Wendy. *In the Ruins of Neoliberalism: The Rise of Antidemocratic Politics in the West.* New York: Columbia University Press, 2019.

Buiter, H. Willem. "'Country Ownership': A Term Whose Time Has Gone." In *Deconstructing Development Discourse: Buzzwords and Fuzzwords*, edited by Andrea Cornwall and Deborah Eade, 223–29. Bourton on Dunsmore: Practical Action Publishing, 2010.

Burchi, Francesco, Markus Loewe, Daniele Malerba, and Julia Leininger. "Disentangling the Relationship between Social Protection and Social Cohesion: Introduction to the Special Issue." *The European Journal of Development Research* 34, no. 3 (2022): 1195–215.

Caraus, Tamara, and Elena Paris, eds. *Migration, Protest Movements and the Politics of Resistance.* New York: Routledge, 2019.

Carpenter, Michael J., and Benjamin Perrier. "Yellow Vests: Anti-austerity, Pro-democracy, and Popular (Not Populist)." *Frontiers in Political Science* 5 (2023): 1037942. doi: 10.3389/fpos.2023.1037942.

Chan, Joseph, Ho-Pong To, and Elaine Chan. "Reconsidering Social Cohesion: Developing a Definition and Analytical Framework for Empirical Research." *Social Indicators Research* 75 (2006): 273–302.

Chandhoke, Neera. *State and Civil Society.* New Delhi: Sage Publications, 1995.

Chandhoke, Neera. "Civil Society." In *Deconstructing Development Discourse: Buzzwords and Fuzzwords*, edited by Andrea Cornwall and Deborah Eade, 175–84. Bourton on Dunsmore: Practical Action Publishing, 2010.

Cho, Seongha. "Economic Conditions and Social Cohesion: An Analysis of French European Social Survey Data." *French Politics* 20, no. 1 (2022): 25–52.

Cohen, L. Jean, and Andrew Arato. *Civil Society and Political Theory.* Cambridge MA: The MIT Press, 1994.

Cooper, Davina. *Feeling Like a State: Desire, Denial, and the Recasting of Authority.* Durham: Duke University Press, 2019.

Cornwall, Andrea. "Introductory Overview—Buzzwords and Fuzzwords: Deconstructing Development Discourse." In *Deconstructing Development Discourse: Buzzwords and Fuzzwords*, edited by Andrea Cornwall and Deborah Eade, 1–18. Bourton on Dunsmore: Practical Action Publishing, 2010.

Cornwall, Andrea, and Karen Brock. "What Do Buzzwords Do for Development Policy? A Critical Look at 'Participation,' 'Empowerment' and 'Poverty Reduction.'" *Third World Quarterly* 26, no. 7 (2005): 1043–1060.

Dardot, Pierre, and Christian Laval. *The New Way of the World: On Neoliberal Society*, trans. Gregory Elliott. London: Verso, 2013.

Davies, William. *The Limits of Neoliberalism: Authority, Sovereignty and the Logic of Competition.* London: Sage Publications, 2014.

Delhey, Jan, Klaus Boehnke, Georgi Dragolov, Zsófia Ignácz, Mandi Larsen, Jan Lorenz, and Michael Koch. "Social Cohesion and Its Correlates: A Comparison of Western and Asian Societies." *Comparative Sociology* 17, no. 3–4 (2018): 426–55.

Della Porta, Donatella. *How Social Movements Can Save Democracy: Democratic Innovations from Below.* Cambridge: Polity 2020.

Dobbernack, Jan. *The Politics of Social Cohesion in Germany, France and the United Kingdom.* Basingstoke: Palgrave Macmillan, 2014.

Doornbos, Martin. *Social Research and Policy in the Development Arena.* Basingstoke: Palgrave Macmillan, 2015.

Dragolov, Georgi, Zsófia Ignácz, Jan Lorenz, Jan Delhey, and Klaus Boehnke. *The Social Cohesion Radar: Measuring Common Ground—An International Comparison of Social Cohesion.* Gütersloh: Bertelsmann Stiftung, 2013.

Dragolov, Georgi, Zsófia S. Ignácz, Jan Lorenz, Jan Delhey, Klaus Boehnke, and Kai Unzicker. *Social Cohesion in the Western World: What Holds Societies Together: Insights from the Social Cohesion Radar.* Dordrecht: Springer, 2016.

Duffield, Mark. *Development, Security and Unending War: Governing the World of Peoples.* Cambridge: Polity Press, 2007.

Eade, Deborah. "Preface." In *Deconstructing Development Discourse: Buzzwords and Fuzzwords*, edited by Andrea Cornwall and Deborah Eade, vii–x. Bourton on Dunsmore: Practical Action Publishing, 2010.

Escobar, Arturo. *Pluriversal Politics: The Real and the Possible.* Durham, NC: Duke University Press, 2020.

Esping-Andersen, Gøsta. *The Three Worlds of Welfare Capitalism.* Cambridge: Polity Press, 1990.

Fenger, Menno. "Deconstructing Social Cohesion: Towards an Analytical Frame for Assessing Social Cohesion Policies." *Corvinus Journal of Sociology and Social Policy* 3, no. 2 (2012): 39–54.

Fine, Ben. "Social Capital." In *Deconstructing Development Discourse: Buzzwords and Fuzzwords*, edited by Andrea Cornwall and Deborah Eade. Bourton on Dunsmore: Practical Action Publishing, 2010.

Fine, Ben. *Theories of Social Capital: Researchers Behaving Badly.* London: Pluto, 2010.

Finlayson, Lorna. *The Political Is Political: Conformity and the Illusion of Dissent in Contemporary Political Philosophy.* Lanham: Rowman & Littlefield, 2015.

Firth, Rhiannon. *Disaster Anarchy: Mutual Aid and Radical Action.* London: Pluto Press, 2022.

Fitzpatrick, Suzanne, and Anwen Jones. "Pursuing Social Justice or Social Cohesion?: Coercion in Street Homelessness Policies in England." *Journal of Social Policy* 34, no. 3 (2005): 389–406.

Fonseca, Xavier, Stephan Lukosch, and Frances Brazier. "Social Cohesion Revisited: A New Definition and How to Characterise It." *Innovation: The European Journal of Social Science Research* 32, no. 2 (2018): 231–53.

Forrest, Ray, and Ade Kearns. "Social Cohesion, Social Capital and the Neighbourhood." *Urban Studies* 38, no. 12 (2001): 2125–43.

Friedman, Milton. *Capitalism and Freedom.* Chicago: University of Chicago Press, 2002[1962].

Gallie, B. Walter. "Essentially Contested Concepts." *Proceedings of the Aristotelian Society* 56, no. 1 (1956): 167–98.

Geuss, Raymond. *The Idea of a Critical Theory: Habermas and the Frankfurt School.* Cambridge: Cambridge University Press, 1981.

Gilbert, Jeremy. "An Aesthetics of Solidarity: Collective Becoming after Neoliberalism." In *Crisis and Communitas*, edited by Dorota Sajewska and Małgorzata Sugiera, 21–39. Abingdon: Routledge, 2023.

Green, Andy, and Jan Germen Janmaat. *Regimes of Social Cohesion: Societies and the Crisis of Globalisation.* Basingstoke: Palgrave Macmillan, 2011.

Green, Duncan. "Social Cohesion—There's a Lot More to It Than the OECD Version." Oxfam, 2012. https://frompoverty.oxfam.org.uk/social-cohesion-a-lot-more-interesting-than-the-oecd-makes-out/.

Gregersen, J. Kasper. "Assessing the Glue That Holds Society Together: Social Cohesion Arguments in Liberal Democracy." *Tidsskrift for Medier, Erkendelse Og Formidling* 1, no. 2 (2013): 78–94.

Holtug, Nils. *The Politics of Social Cohesion: Immigration, Community, and Justice.* Oxford: Oxford University Press, 2021.

Honig, Bonnie. *Public Things: Democracy in Disrepair.* New York: Fordham University Press, 2017.

Illner, Peer. *Disasters and Social Reproduction: Crisis Response between the State and Community.* London: Pluto Press, 2020.

Ingram, D. James. "Cosmopolitanism from Below: Universalism as Contestation." *Critical Horizons* 17, no. 1 (2016): 66–78.

IPSOS. *Social Cohesion in the Pandemic Age: A Global Perspective,* 2020.

Jaffe, Aaron. *Social Reproduction Theory and the Socialist Horizon.* London: Pluto Press, 2020.

Janmaat, Jan Germen. "Social Cohesion as a Real-life Phenomenon: Assessing the Explanatory Power of the Universalist and Particularist Perspectives." *Social Indicators Research* 100 (2011): 61–83.

Jenson, Jane. *Mapping Social Cohesion: The State of Canadian Research,* Study No. F/03. Ottawa: Canadian Policy Research Networks, 1998.

Kasza, J. Gregory. "The Illusion of Welfare 'Regimes.'" *Journal of Social Policy* 31, no. 2 (2002): 271–87.

King, Natasha. *No Borders: The Politics of Immigration Control and Resistance.* London: Zed Books, 2016.

Koch, Max, Jayeon Lindellee, and Johanna Alkan Olsson. "Beyond the Growth Imperative and Neoliberal Doxa: Expanding Alternative Societal Spaces through Deliberative Citizen Forums on Needs Satisfaction." *real-world economics review* 96 (2021): 168–83. http://www.paecon.net/PAEReview/issue96/Koch-et-al96.pdf.

Kropotkin, Peter. *Mutual Aid: A Factor of Evolution.* London: Freedom Press, 2009[1902].

Lalot, Fanny, Dominic Abrams, Jo Bradwood, Kaya Davies Hayon, and Isobel Platts-Dunn. "The Social Cohesion Investment: Communities That Invested in Integration Programmes Are Showing Greater Social Cohesion in the Midst of the COVID-19 Pandemic." *Journal of Community & Applied Social Psychology* 32, no. 3 (2022): 536–54. https://doi.org/10.1002/casp.2522.

Laruffa, Francesco. "Studying the Relationship between Social Policy Promotion and Neoliberalism: The Case of Social Investment." *New Political Economy* 27, no. 3 (2022): 473–89.

Leininger, Julia, Francesco Burchi, Charlotte Fiedler, Karina Moss, Daniel Nowack, Armin von Schiller, Christoph Sommer, Christoph Strupat, and Sebastian Ziaja. *Social Cohesion: A New Definition and a Proposal for Its Measurement in Africa.* Bonn: Deutsches Institut für Entwicklungspolitik, 2021.

Lockley-Scott, Anna. "Towards a Critique of Fundamental British Values: The Case of the Classroom." *Journal of Beliefs & Values* 40, no. 3 (2019): 354–67.

Lynch, Kathleen. *Care and Capitalism.* Cambridge: Polity, 2022.

MacIntyre, Alasdair. "Politics, Philosophy and the Common Good." In *The MacIntyre Reader*, edited by Kelvin Knight, 235–52. South Bend: University of Notre Dame Press, 1998.

Maloutas, Thomas, and Maro Pantelidou Malouta. "The Glass Menagerie of Urban Governance and Social Cohesion: Concepts and Stakes/ Concepts as Stakes." *International Journal of Urban and Regional Research* 28, no. 2 (2004): 449–65.

Manca, Anna Rita. "Social Cohesion." In *Encyclopedia of Quality of Life and Well-Being Research*, edited by Alex C. Michalos, 6026–28. Dordrecht: Springer, 2014. https://doi.org/10.1007/978-94-007-0753-5_2739.

Mannheim, Karl. *Ideology and Utopia.* London: Routledge and Kegan Paul, 1960.

Maxwell, Judith. *Social Dimensions of Economic Growth.* Alberta: University of Alberta, 1996.

Merino, Roger. "An Alternative to 'Alternative Development'?: Buen Vivir and Human Development in Andean Countries." *Oxford Development Studies* 44, no. 3 (2016): 271–86. http://dx.doi.org/10.1080/13600818.2016.1144733.

Monticelli, Lara. "On the Necessity of Prefigurative Politics." *Thesis Eleven* 167, no. 1 (2021): 99–118. https://doi.org/10.1177/07255136211056992.

Moustakas, Louis. "A Bibliometric Analysis of Research on Social Cohesion from 1994–2020." *Publications* 10, no. 1 (2022). https:/doi.org/10.3390/publications10010005.

Neocleous, Mark. "Resisting Resilience." *Radical Philosophy* 178 (2013). https://www.radicalphilosophy.com/commentary/resisting-resilience.

Nietzsche, Friedrich. *On the Genealogy of Morals and Ecce Homo*, trans. Walter Kaufmann. New York: Vintage Books, 1989.

Ostrom, Elinor. *Governing the Commons.* Cambridge: Cambridge University Press, 2015.

Pahl, E. Ray. "The Search for Social Cohesion: From Durkheim to the European Commission." *European Journal of Sociology* 32, no. 2 (1991): 345–60. DOI:10.1017/S0003975600006305.

Phillips, Anne. *Unconditional Equals.* Princeton: Princeton University Press, 2021.

Pickard, Miguel. "Reflections on Relationships: The Nature of Partnership According to Five NGOs in Southern Mexico." In *Deconstructing Development Discourse: Buzzwords and Fuzzwords*, edited by Andrea Cornwall and Deborah Eade, 135–42. Bourton on Dunsmore: Practical Action Publishing, 2010.

Putnam, Robert. *Bowling Alone.* New York: Simon & Schuster, 2000.

Putnam, Robert, and Lewis M. Feldstein. *Better Together: Restoring the American Community.* New York: Simon & Schuster, 2004.

Raekstad, Paul, and Sofa Saio Gradin. *Prefigurative Politics: Building Tomorrow Today.* Cambridge: Polity, 2020.

Rappleye, Jeremy, Hikaru Komatsu, Yukiko Uchida, Kuba Krys, and Hazel Markus. "'Better Policies for Better Lives'?: Constructive Critique of the OECD's (Mis)measure of Student Well-being." *Journal of Education Policy* 35, no. 2 (2019): 258–82. DOI: 10.1080/02680939.2019.1576923.

Rawls, John, *Political Liberalism.* New York: Columbia University Press, 1995.

Rist, Gilbert. *The History of Development: From Western Origins to Global Faith*, trans. Patrick Camiller. New York: Zed Books, 2008.

Rist, Gilbert. "Development as a Buzzword." In *Deconstructing Development Discourse: Buzzwords and Fuzzwords*, edited by Andrea Cornwall and Deborah Eade, 19–27. Bourton on Dunsmore: Practical Action Publishing, 2010.

Russell, Bertrand. *Reith Lectures 1948: Authority and the Individual*, "Lecture 1: Social Cohesion and Human Nature." Accessed December 4, 2022. http://downloads.bbc.co.uk/rmhttp/radio4/transcripts/1948_reith1.pdf.

Sager, Alex. "Reclaiming Cosmopolitanism through Migrant Protests." In *Migration, Protest Movements and the Politics of Resistance*, edited by Tamara Caraus and Elena Paris, 171–85. New York: Routledge, 2019.

Savage, Mike. *The Return of Inequality: Social Change and the Weight of the Past.* Cambridge, MA: Harvard University Press, 2021.

Schiefer, David, and Jolanda van der Noll. "The Essentials of Social Cohesion: A Literature Review.'" *Social Indicators Research* 132 (2017): 579–603.

Scott, C. James. *Seeing Like a State: How Certain Schemes to Improve the Human Condition Have Failed.* New Haven: Yale University Press, 1999.

Sen, Amartya. *The Standard of Living.* Cambridge: Cambridge University Press, 1987.

Smith, S. Stephen, and Jessica Kulynych. "It May Be Social, But Why Is It Capital? The Social Construction of Social Capital and the Politics of Language." *Politics and Society* 30, no.1 (2002): 149–86.

Spade, Dean. *Mutual Aid: Building Solidarity During This Crisis and the Next.* London and New York: Verso, 2020.

Standing, Guy. "Social Protection." In *Deconstructing Development Discourse: Buzzwords and Fuzzwords*, edited by Andrea Cornwall and Deborah Eade, 53–67. Bourton on Dunsmore: Practical Action Publishing, 2010.

Stiglitz, E. Joseph, Amartya Sen, and Jean-Paul Fitoussi. *Report by the Commission on the Measurement of Economic Performance and Social Progress.* 2009.

Sung-Geun, Kim. "Measuring Regional Social Cohesion by Objective Indices: The Case of Korea." *International Journal of Community Well-Being* 5, no. 3 (2022): 1–29.

Swain, Dan, Petr Urban, Catherine Malabou, and Petr Kouba, eds. *Unchaining Solidarities: On Mutual Aid and Anarchism with Catherine Malabou.* Lanham: Rowman & Littlefield, 2021.

Taylor, Katherine Selena, Sheri Longboat, and Rupert Quentin Grafton. "Whose Rules? A Water Justice Critique of the OECD's 12 Principles on Water Governance." *Water* 11, no. 4, 809 (2019). DOI: 10.3390/w11040809.

Telleria, Juan. *Deconstructing Human Development: From the Washington Consensus to the 2030 Agenda.* New York: Routledge, 2021.

Thompson, Matthew. "What's So New about New Municipalism?" *Progress in Human Geography* 45, no. 2 (2021): 317–42.

Tronto, Joan. *Caring Democracy: Markets, Equality, and Justice.* New York: New York University Press, 2013.

Union of Education Norway. *From Inspiration to Uniformity? 20 Years of OECD in the Field of Early Childhood Education and Care.* 2020.

van de Sande, Matthijs. *Prefigurative Democracy: Protest, Social Movements and the Political Institution of Society.* Edinburgh: University of Edinburgh Press, 2022.

Williams, Rowan. *Solidarity: Necessary Fiction or Metaphysical Given. Third Gillian Rose Memorial Lecture.* Kingston: CRMEP Books, 2023.

Wimmer, Andreas, and Nina Glick Schiller. "Methodological Nationalism, the Social Sciences, and the Study of Migration: An Essay in Historical Epistemology." *International Migration Review* 37, no. 3 (2003): 576–610.

Wittgenstein, Ludwig. *Philosophical Investigations*, trans. G. E. M. Anscombe. Oxford: Blackwell, 1967.

Wolff, Robert Paul, Barrington Moore Jr., and Herbert Marcuse. *A Critique of Pure Tolerance.* London: Cape Editions, 1969.

World Economic Forum. *The Global Risks Report 2022: 17th Edition.* Geneva: World Economic Forum, 2022.

Yıldız, Ümit. "An Anti-racist Reading of the Notion of 'Fundamental British Values.'" *Prism* 3, no. 2 (2021): 91–107.

Index

activation, 43, 48, 53
activism, xviii, 79–80, 85, 90
advocacy, 65
Africa, 65–66, 68
anarchism, 85
Arab region, 65–67, 70, 77
asylum seekers, 47
attitudes, 8, 12, 19, 202–4, 33–35, 55, 64, 77, 85, 98n9
autonomy, national, 69

belonging, 2, 10, 16, 20–22, 34, 48, 61, 66, 87–88
Bertelsmann Stiftung, 21, 98–99n11
borders, 15–17, 78, 88
bottom-up approach, 51, 87
buen vivir, 87
buzzword, xiii, 54–55, 80–83, 90. See also fuzzword

capabilities: human, 61; individual, 45–46, 64; approach, 61, 76
capital: social, 11, 14–15, 44, 46, 53, 55, 61–62, 64, 66, 75–76, 80, 97n, 101n60, 102n66; human, 44–46, 53, 64; as wealth, 84
capitalism, 30, 35–36, 85, 115n38
care, xiv, 116n

the Caribbean, 58, 63, 72, 83
charity, 29–30, 49, 58, 85, 88–89
citizenship, 2, 15, 22, 46, 53, 55, 64–65, 88
civil liberties, 61
civil society, 3, 29–31, 34, 48–49, 62, 65, 76, 80–81, 84, 102n102–3
climate crisis. See crisis, climate
Club of Madrid, 62
coercion, 8, 33–34, 102n71
coexistence, 71
colonialism, 67, 69, 77
common good, 12, 16, 22, 29–32, 88–90, 116n52, 116–17n58
community: as value, 9, 55; groups and activists, xvii, 29–30, 79–80; political, 7, 14, 22, 44, 88–89
competition, 59–60, 85
competitiveness, economic, 45–46, 52, 78
conditionality (of economic aid), 63
conflict, xi, 2, 36, 52, 63, 66, 77, 88, 90; management, 48–49; resolution, 62; violent, 40, 64
connectedness, 22, 25, 101n60, 102n66
consensus, 54, 59–60, 76; opposed to coercion, 8, 33, 102n71; normative, 11, 25, 61

contestation, xvii, 23, 65, 68, 71–73, 80–83, 89. *See also* essentially contested concepts
cooperation, social, 6, 17, 19, 21, 32, 84, 88–89
Council of Europe, xvi, 20, 47–56, 57, 105n52, 114n22
country ownership, 78, 112n110
COVID-19 pandemic, xi, xiv, 51, 85, 99n12
crisis xiv, 75; climate xi, 79; financial 44–45, 53, 61, 83; sense of 4, 54, 67
critical theory, xiii, 112n10

decline, xv, 4–5, 17, 36–37, 52, 95n18
definition, xii-xiii, 20, 23, 81, 110n75; down-to-earth, 80; normative vs. non-normative, 12–14, 27; particularist vs. universalist, xv, 6–8, 18–22, 24–26, 33–38, 80, 96n37; philosophical problems of, 6; substantive vs. formalist, 10–11, 27
democracy, 11, 30, 48, 51, 53, 59–60, 63–64, 71–72, 82–84, 90. *See also* liberal democratic societies, contestation
democratic deficit, 4, 63
democratic deliberation, xvii, 72, 79–80, 88–90
demographic change, 36, 59
depoliticization, xvi, 29–33, 38, 55, 71–73, 76, 80–82, 89
development: international, xii, xiv, xvi, 11, 21, 24, 57–73, 77, 78, 86–87; personal, 2, 49, 64; human, 27, 69, 71, 87; economic, 28, 40–1, 43, 51, 61, 70; sustainable, 61–62, 77
dignity, 26, 47–49, 71
disabled people, 42, 53
disadvantaged groups, 40, 43, 47
discrimination, 49
disintegration, 47, 54, 60, 94–95n14
disparities, 2, 41–3, 49–50, 52, 54, 65–66
dissent, 11, 77. *See also* consensus
diversity, 11–12, 24–26, 36, 41, 69, 71, 86–87; acceptance of 8, 10–11, 22, 24–26, 27, 31, 65, 86–87, 100n31
domination, 79, 84
Durkheim, Emile 3, 14, 25–26, 84

Eastern Europe, 40, 102n62
economic imperative (social cohesion as an), 41, 46
economic efficiency, 2, 41–43, 51, 56, 61
economic flexibility, 4, 59, 67
economic reform, 59, 70
economic modernization, 4
economic domination, 84
economy, 30, 42–43, 45, 48, 59, 62; knowledge 27–28, 42; market, 59; shadow 29
education, 27, 35–36, 52, 62
efficiency. *See* economic efficiency
egalitarianism, 13, 35, 84, 100n29
elderly people, 51
employment, xvi, 34–35, 40–48, 52, 59, 61–64, 67, 75, 83, 105n74, 109n46
empowerment, 45, 51, 82
environment: social, 61; natural, xi, 51, 61. *See also* crisis, climate
equality, 8, 10–11, 14, 24, 27, 35, 72, 81, 83–84, 90, 100n38; of opportunity, 23, 26, 46, 99n22
erosion of social cohesion, xi-xii, 93n4. *See also* decline
essentially contested concepts, 9, 81, 114n21
ethnic minorities, 24, 47, 53, 64
Eurofound, 5, 12, 21, 28, 40, 83, 99n12
European Commission, 45
European Committee for Social Cohesion, 48, 51
European Social Fund, 45
European Social Charter, 52
European Union, xvi, 20, 39–46, 52–56, 57–58, 76–77

exclusion, social, xvi, 12, 17, 26–27, 31, 35, 42–50, 52, 56, 59, 61, 63–66, 70, 75, 79, 84–86. *See also* inclusion
exploitation, 30, 79, 84, 101n60

fairness, 10, 22, 26, 100n29
faith: in democracy, 11; religious 26, 65
family, 1, 25, 47–48
fraternity, 3, 13, 33, 84, 114n21
freedom, 10, 35, 49, 60
French Republican Tradition, 17, 34, 94–95n14
forced displacement, 111n106
fuzzword, 54–55, 75–83

gender, 35, 65, 84
German Institute of Development and Sustainability, 77
German International Development Agency, 21
Gilets Jaunes, 30, 77
globalization, 4, 36
glue (as metaphor), 5, 70
good life, conceptions of, 4, 25, 55, 76
growth: economic, xiv, 4, 13, 34, 40–46, 52, 56, 60–63, 78–79, 108n25; sustainable, 44–45, 63

health 28, 61
healthcare 52, 105n74
history: end of 4, 54, 60; of colonialism/imperialism, 70, 77; social cohesion in, 1, 23
holding together, xii, xiv, 2, 7–8, 10–11, 13–14, 17, 28, 37, 54–55, 77, 85, 94n9
housing policy, 36, 52, 105n
human resources, 43. *See also* capital, human

identity: national, 26; shared, 1, 8, 11, 21, 64, 88, 94–95n14
ideology: in critical sense, 78–79, 100n40, 102n71, 113n13, 114n25; in descriptive sense, 30, 32, 35–37, 54, 65, 76; smuggled in, 32, 48, 56, 89; traditional, 54, 76
immigration. *See* migration
imperialism, 70
inclusion, 17, 61, 106n93;as related to cohesion, xvi, 45–6, 50, 52–56, 61–64, 66, 75–76, 82; as extension of rights, 48, 50, 52–56, 61–64; labor market, 52, 64, 76; as identified with activation, 53
income: basic, 54, 72; inequality of, 10, 35, 59, 62, 83–84; redistribution of, 36
indicators of social cohesion, 8, 10, 22, 29–31, 35, 43–46, 49, 66–67, 100n29, 100n39
individualistic scenario, 60
inequality, 2, 4, 8, 11, 27, 34, 36, 46, 62–64, 79, 83–84; of wealth 83; return of 83; visceral 84; income. *See* income, inequality of
insecurity, 46, 59
institutions, 7–8, 19, 28, 31, 33–35, 77–78; democratic, 11, 63; international, 58–72, 90; public, xii-xiv, 15–17, 21, 29, 34, 60–62, 72, 98n9; trust in, xi, 22, 66
integration: economic, 62; European, 41; social, 44, 48
isolation, 46

justice: redistributive, 82; social. *See* social justice

labour market, 36, 45–46, 59
Laeken Indicators, 44
Latin America, 30, 58, 63, 72, 83
legitimacy, 10, 61, 63, 66, 71, 73; normative, xii, xvi, 54, 68, 72, 77; scientific, 17, 38, 68, 72
liberal democratic societies, 11–12, 102n64
liberal values, 4, 26, 29–31, 55, 69, 77
liberal regime of social cohesion, 34–37

marginalisation, 54, 61
market: labor, 34–36, 41–46, 48, 52, 56, 59, 64, 75–76; free, 34, 48, 59, 64, 82, 103n. *See also* social market regimes
Marxism, 85–86
metaphor, 5, 9, 15, 69, 78, 89
methodological nationalism, 16–17, 22, 78, 88, 103n85
migration, 16–17, 24, 27, 29–30, 36, 40, 78, 86–88, 103n1
monitoring of social cohesion, 43–44, 46, 62
multiculturalism, 4, 26, 88, 103n1
municipal government, 50, 90
mutual aid, 85–86

nationalism, 16. *See also* methodological nationalism
naturalization: of social cohesion, 55; of the nation state, 16
neoliberalism, xiv, 52–53, 75–76, 89–91, 102–3n84, 112n4, 116–17n58
networks: digital, 44; social, 15, 22, 44, 49, 51, 61, 66
networked society, 44
neutralization (of criticism), 77–82
NGOs, xii, 58
normativity, xv, 2–3, 10–14, 23–28, 32–33, 55, 68, 72, 76–77, 94n9, 100n29, 102n66, 102n71
normative overdetermination, xv, 28, 32, 37, 55, 58, 77

OECD, xvi, 4, 5, 21, 57–63, 67, 70, 72, 76–77, 108n9, 108n25, 109n46
ontological realism, xv, 5, 9, 22, 76, 95n25
operationalizable concept, xiv, 5–6, 15, 37, 43, 46, 52–56, 68, 81

participation, 10, 15, 21, 38, 44, 50, 53, 55, 61, 64, 66, 76, 89–90; active 43, 59, 64; as buzzword 82; civic xvi, 22, 29–32, 48–49, 52, 62, 88, 101n57, 101n60; labor market 46, 53; political 15, 21, 30, 101n57
particularism. *See* definitions, universalist vs. particularist
peace, 45, 65–66, 71; social 49, 62
peer pressure, 63
pluralism, xv, 2, 4, 11–14, 22–23, 27, 55, 60, 65, 86–88, 90, 113n13
pluriverse, 87
policymakers, xii, 3, 5, 9, 11, 14, 19, 20, 23, 32, 37, 69, 79, 91, 98n10, 101n45, 104n27
political community. *See* community, political
political participation. *See* participation, political
politicization. *See* depoliticization
positivism, 95n25
poverty, 8, 41–50, 52, 58, 61–64, 79, 104n27
prefigurative politics, 85
process, social cohesion as a, 2, 6–7, 20, 50, 66, 96n31
productivity, 41–43
progress: economic, 41–43, 51–52, 79; human, 1, 27–29, 57, 69–70, 72, 79; social, 41–43, 62,
prosperity, economic, xiv, 4, 34, 41, 60, 101n45, 108n25
protest, 88

quality of life, 2–3, 40–44

race, 1, 36, 47, 84
realism, ontological. *See* ontological realism
recognition, 61, 85
redistribution, 11, 35–36, 82–83
reform: economic, 4, 59, 63–64, 70, 76; vs. revolution, 30
refugees, 40, 47
regimes of social cohesion, 8, 33–37
regulative ideal, 13, 49, 55

reification of social cohesion 55, 86. *See also* naturalization, ontological realism
resilience, 79, 112n4, 113n14, 116n56
responsibility: for social cohesion, 49–50, 58; individual, 51, 53, 60
rights: human, 47–49, 64, 71; property, 34; social, xvi, 47–51, 54–56, 64; universal, 60

safety net, 64
satisfaction: job, 40, 66; life, 8, 28, 62, 66
security, 25, 44, 46, 60, 62, 66, 71; democratic, 48; European, 47, 51; social, 48–49, 64
sexuality, 24, 65,
shared goals, 16, 44, 89
Social Cohesion Radar, 5, 21–33, 35, 83, 88, 98n10
social democratic regime of social cohesion, 34–36
social fabric, 9, 47, 60, 67–68, 84, 108n25
social fragmentation, 60
social harmony, 48–49
social ills, 4, 49, 54
social justice, 2, 10, 26, 43, 46–47, 54, 63, 81–82, 100n38, 106n93
social market regime of social cohesion, 34–37
social mobility, 61–63
social movements, xiv, xvii, 79, 88, 90
social protection, 41, 45, 54, 62–64, 105n74
social relations: as component of social cohesion, 22–24, 65–66; treated instrumentally, xiv, 28–29, 32, 53, 76, 86
social research, xvii, 3–6, 9, 18–20, 37–38, 79–80, 90
social rules, 22, 88
social services, 49
society: cohesive, 3, 6, 10, 15, 21, 28, 33, 39, 45–46, 48, 50, 55, 62, 77,

99n20; dual, 41; knowledge, 44; good, 7, 13, 26, 30, 32; well-ordered, 61, 77
solidarity, xi, xiv, 3–4, 11, 14, 17, 22, 34, 47–51, 82, 84–91; active vs. passive, 41, 43, 52, 76; organic and mechanical, 24–26
stability, social. *See* social stability
state of affairs, social cohesion as a, 6–7, 20, 22, 31, 50
status quo: maintaining, 62; stabilizing, xiii, 56, 77–79, 82; taking for granted, xvi, 53, 78, 90, 113n13
Stiglitz-Sen-Fitoussi Commission, 62
stability, xi-xii, 47–48, 52, 62, 70, 78, 85; political, 13, 31; social, 3, 14, 37, 48–49
substance metaphor, xii-xiii, xvii, 2, 5, 9, 76, 82, 86. *See also* ontological realism.
sustainability, xii, 45, 67–68, 77, 107n, 112n4; of welfare systems, 59

thick vs. thin conceptions, xii, xv, 2–3, 8, 11, 18, 67–68, 71, 76, 94n9
third-way politics, 4–5, 75
threats: to social cohesion, 2, 4, 7, 27, 36–37, 40–43, 48, 51–52, 59, 62, 84, 87–8; social cohesion discourse as response to, xv-xvii, 4–5, 37, 51–2, 54, 56, 77. *See also* decline
tolerance, xv, 11–12, 22–26, 29, 32, 35–36, 65, 71, 77, 86, 100n40. *See also* diversity, acceptance. *See also* pluralism
trust: as component of social cohesion, 10–11, 13, 20, 22, 24, 26, 31, 34–37, 44, 87, 90; institutional, xi, 8, 15, 22, 36, 61–62, 65–66; personal, 8, 22, 36, 44, 61–62, 65–66

UN, xvi, 63–73, 108n9–10
UNDP, 64–71, 87, 110n75
unemployment, 4, 35, 42–43, 47–8, 52, 59–62, 77, 104n27

universalism. *See* definitions, universalist vs. particularist
USAID, 65, 113n14
utopia, 85, 114n25

value: intrinsic, 13–14, 43, 52, 55, 107n8; instrumental, 13–14, 28–33, 43, 52, 55, 68, 76–77, 82, 86, 107n8
values: first- vs. second-order, 11–12, 25–26, 28; non-material, 51; universal cultural, 69, 87; substantive, xii, xv, 2, 10–14, 17–18, 43, 55, 76, 78, 86, 100n29. *See also* normativity. *See also* definition, normative vs. non-normative. *See also* definition, substantive vs. formalist
vertical vs. horizontal dimensions of social cohesion, 20, 29, 66, 88

volunteering, 29, 49, 53, 88–89, 101n60
vulnerable groups, 42, 49, 51, 64, 66

wealth, 8, 10, 27, 35, 47, 60–62, 83–84
welfare, 25, 34–6, 49–53, 59
welfare state, 4, 36, 42, 59, 67, 75
well-being, 2–3, 8–10, 13, 28–29, 42, 45–6, 50–4, 61–3, 67, 83, 87, 108n; economic 42, 61, 108n25; human 61; social 83; subjective 28–29, 62. *See also* capabilities approach
workfare, 53–4
World Bank, 97n68, 107n8, 110n75
World Economic Forum, xi, 83, 93n4, 113n14

xenophobia, 47

Zapatistas, 87

About the Authors

Dan Swain is a researcher at the Institute of Philosophy of the Czech Academy of Sciences and assistant professor in the Department of Humanities of the Czech University of Life Sciences Prague. He is the author of *None So Fit to Break the Chains: Marx's Ethics of Self-Emancipation* (2019/2020) and *Alienation: An Introduction to Marx's Theory* (2012) and co-editor of *Unchaining Solidarity: On Mutual Aid and Anarchism with Catherine Malabou* (2021). As well as Marx and Marxism, his research focuses on the theory and practice of social movements, radical democracy and utopianism.

Petr Urban is a senior researcher at the Institute of Philosophy of the Czech Academy of Sciences. His research focuses on political theory of care, applied ethics, and phenomenology. His work has appeared in journals such as *Frontiers in Psychology*; *Ethics and Social Welfare*; *Environmental Philosophy*; *Horizon: Studies in Phenomenology*; *Philosophies*; and *Humana Mente*. He is a co-editor of *Care Ethics, Democratic Citizenship and the State* (2020); *Unchaining Solidarity: On Mutual Aid and Anarchism with Catherine Malabou* (2021); and *Play and Democracy: Philosophical Perspectives* (2022).

Milton Keynes UK
Ingram Content Group UK Ltd.
UKHW011028030324
438653UK00002B/11